Butterflies of Arizona

A Photographic Guide

Other books by Bob Stewart
from West Coast Lady Press

Common Butterflies of California

Butterflies of Arizona
A Photographic Guide

Bob Stewart, Priscilla Brodkin & Hank Brodkin

✦

West Coast Lady Press
2001

Printed in Hong Kong Through Colour Books Production Limited

10 9 8 7 6 5 4 3 2

West Coast Lady Press
645 Elizabeth Drive
Arcata, CA 95521

On the front cover: **Gray Hairstreak**

On the back cover: **Dull Firetip**, *above;*
Arizona Hairstreak, *below*

Table of Contents

*This book is dedicated
to the butterflies
of Arizona.*

Preface and Acknowledgements

Until the relatively recent past, collection of butterfly specimens has been the only possible way to document species occurrence, distribution and time of flight. Patient observation and rearing of larvae has helped our knowledge of host plants, although there are still some species about which we lack this knowledge.

The older field guides were prepared for collectors and usually featured drawings or photographs of mounted butterflies, usually showing the dorsal side only. All the collector would have to do to make an identification was to compare his spread specimen with the illustration.

In the 1980s, in New York, a group of birders—some of whom happened to be butterfly enthusiasts—started directing their birding skills toward butterflies, mainly trying to identify them with binoculars. Out of this beginning, under the guidance of Jeffrey Glassberg, the North American Butterfly Association (NABA) was formed and, with it, the new, rapidly growing hobby of butterfly watching—butterflying. The use of close-focus binoculars and macro photography (see page 4) has opened a whole new world to thousands of people.

It became clear early on that the old-style field guide was not very useful for identification purposes. Live butterflies in nature are not seen spread flat, and many species, such as Sulphurs and Hairstreaks, most often perch with their wings closed. In response, a whole new kind of field guide was born. As early as 1981, Robert Pyle, another early champion of butterflying, wrote the *Audubon Society Field Guide to North American Butterflies* in which all the illustrations were photographs of living butterflies.

Collecting butterflies is still a legitimate scientific and educational endeavor, and we hope that many collectors will find this book useful. *The Butterflies of Arizona*, however, was produced mainly for the butterfly observer who wants to enjoy the beauty of these creatures while causing a minimum of disturbance. We hope that the butterflyer will benefit from this book's photographs, taken opportunely under natural conditions, and will encourage others to participate in this fascinating and rewarding avocation. A word of caution: some species, especially some Skippers, will be very difficult, if not impossible, to identify just by observing. We hope that in the future (just as sharp young birders were able to discover ways to differentiate the supposedly unidentifiable Empidonax flycatchers), some of you using this book will push the identification envelope forward.

Bob Stewart, a professional naturalist, who has previously worked at the Point Reyes Bird Observatory and Marin County Parks and Open Space Department in California, where his natural history courses have become legendary, started photographing butterflies in 1992 in order to learn to identify them. Ray Peterson, Jim Brock, and Rich Bailowitz have inspired and helped him in the field. In 1997 he published *Common Butterflies of California*. Bob has traveled extensively in Mexico, Central and South America, and in Kenya. For the past three years he has lived with his wife, artist Kathie Bunnell, in Patagonia, Arizona.

The Brodkins' interest in butterflies had its inception in California, where, some years ago, they were initiated into the world of diurnal Lepidoptera by fellow birders Kimball Garret and NABA Director Fred Heath. In 1996, they attended the semiannual meeting of NABA in Sierra Vista, Arizona, and were so struck by the diversity and abundance of butterflies and other life forms—and with the area's biological connection with the neotropics, where they had traveled extensively—that they decided to move permanently to a canyon in the Huachuca Mountains. They have led many field trips in the southeastern Arizona area, and Priscilla has given many butterfly slide presentations to various organizations. In 1999, they helped found the Southeast Arizona Butterfly Association, NABA's only Arizona Chapter. The Brodkins would like to thank several people for accompanying them in the field and otherwise generously sharing their knowledge of Arizona butterflies: Rich Bailowitz, Jim Brock, Wanda Dameron, Doug Danforth, Doug Mullins, and Bruce Walsh.

We are indebted beyond measure to Claire Peaslee, our editor and graphics designer, without whom this book could never have been produced. We thank Jim Brock for reading and making corrections and changes in the manuscript, aiding us in correct identification of the photographs, and enthusiastically sharing his intimate knowledge of Arizona butterflies. Andrew Warren graciously helped in the identification of the Skipper photographs. We also thank botanists Richard S. Felger and Michael F. Wilson of the Drylands Institute in Tucson for editing and putting the latest scientific names to our extensive host plant section. Carl Olson of the University of Arizona identified the insect predators and parasitoids. Kathie Bunnell's experienced artistic eye was invaluable in choosing and color balancing the 550 or so photographs that are used in the book. Bob is indebted to Kathie for her practical, physical, mental and emotional help during the development of the book. Liz Tuomi proofread the final manuscript.

Several people generously shared their photographs to complete the book: they include Jim Brock, Jeff Glassberg, Doug Danforth, Paul Opler and Evi Buckner, Rick and Nora Bowers, Jerry McWilliams, Larry Sansone, Cathy Burgess, Robert Cambell, and Mike Quinn.

From a casual conversation on one butterfly-filled day in Garden Canyon, the authors realized that this book could become a reality. We sincerely hope you will enjoy reading and using it (especially *using* it) as much as we have enjoyed producing it.

Bob Stewart, Priscilla Brodkin and Hank Brodkin
March 22, 2001

Introduction

In the United States, Arizona is second only to Texas in its number of butterfly species. As of this writing, some 330 species have occurred here. The reason for this is the state's great diversity of habitats. The western borderlands have the Colorado River Valley, with the Mojave Desert in the northwest. Rocky Mountain and Great Basin affinities with sub-alpine forests and meadows and sagebrush flats enter the state from the north and east, culminating in the Mogollon Rim and the White Mountains. The greatest diversity, however, is in the southeastern part of the state with its Sonoran and Chihuahua Desert influences and the "Sky Island" archipelago that is the northern extension of Mexico's Sierra Madre Occidental. In the counties of Pima, Santa Cruz, Cochise, Pinal and Graham, more than 250 species of butterfly have been documented. It is here that butterflyers search the border canyons— Sycamore, California Gulch, Garden and Guadalupe—during the summer monsoons for rare strays from Mexico. It is here that one can feel the breath of the Neotropics from mid-July into September, when the land turns green and the sun angels in their countless thousands dance and glide through the air, bringing us dreams of those magical lands to the south.

We hope that this book with its beautiful photographs of butterflies will stimulate an interest in seeing and identifying. Identifying means naming, but we know that naming is the natural consequence of being able to distinguish one kind from another. To distinguish, we have to observe carefully. Observing can be the beginning of a pleasurable experience of habitats that are home to plants, birds, and other insects as well as butterflies. Spending time outside in natural habitats, we discover the immediacy and the wonder of organisms that have existed long before human culture began. It is not surprising that some of us develop a passion for butterflies. But that passion can spread beyond mere enjoyment to include all the life that is connected to butterflies. We hope that these pages will enhance your passion for the butterflies wherever you live or travel.

How to use this book

This book has been organized by the following families:

Swallowtails: large butterflies with tails

Whites and Sulphurs: species that are predominantly white or yellow

Hairstreaks: small butterflies that often have tiny tails on the hind wings

Blues: small butterflies with blue upper wings on the males

Coppers: small butterflies that generally have copper-colored upper wings

Metalmarks: small butterflies that generally have metallic-appearing markings and long antennae

Brush-footed Butterflies: a large group of diverse species that appear to have only four legs

Skippers: medium to small brown or blackish butterflies with the antennae clubs bent backwards

For each species a simple, consistent format has been chosen to enable the user to obtain succinct information while referring to the photographs on the opposite page.

The common name is in **bold letters** followed by the *scientific name in italics* and the page number and letter indicating the location of the photograph(s) on the opposite page.

The photographs, as indicated by the letters "**a, b, c, d**" on the text page, are either full-page, two per page, three per page, or four per page—in one of the following formats:

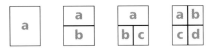

KEY FIELD MARKS: The salient field marks that are distinguishing features for each species are given in **boldface type**. Because butterflies have two front wings and two hind wings, and usually different patterns on the top and bottom of these, abbreviations for these are given in boldface italics (see page 4).

SIZE: The size of the front wing, from the base to the tip, in inches.

ADULTS FLY: The months the adult butterfly is seen.

HOST PLANTS: Listed are some of the plants on which each butterfly species lays eggs and which its larvae will eat. A complete list of host plants with scientific names is given for each species in the Appendix.

RANGE: The general distribution of the species within Arizona (and in which of the surrounding states—California, Nevada, Utah, Colorado, and New Mexico—it is found).

HABITAT: The general habitats in which each species occurs.

SIMILAR SPECIES: The key field marks that distinguish it from other, similar species.

NOTES: Additional information about the species.

Though this book is about butterflies in Arizona many of the species are seen in surrounding states. This information is included after the range is described for Arizona. The number following each state is the percentage of butterflies (not including the Skippers) covered in this book that also occur in the other states.

CA = California   68%
NV = Nevada   67%
UT = Utah   68%
CO = Colorado   74%
NM = New Mexico 84%

The common and scientific names in this book are those used in the *NABA Checklist and English Names of North American Butterflies, Second Edition* by Cassie et al (2001), published by the North American Butterfly Association. A number of subspecies are used in this book. These are denoted by a trinomial, for example, *Chiodes catillus albofasciatus*.

Butterfly Life Cycle

Butterflies deposit their eggs on discrete host plants. Some species lay only on one species of plant, while others may have quite a number of hosts. The egg is only a few millimeters in size; its surface is porous, with about 14,000 holes that allow air but not water to enter. The larva or caterpillar stage hatches from the egg and begins to eat the host plant. The butterfly's larva, like all insects', has an outside skeleton or skin that eventually becomes too small for the growing caterpillar. It sheds this outer skin four or five times as it becomes larger, and three different hormones regulate this molting process. One of these, called juvenile hormone, keeps the larva from developing adult structures. This hormone does not circulate during the last molt, and some adult structures immediately begin to form on the inside of the caterpillar. When the last-stage caterpillar has grown to sufficient size, it wanders off to enter the pupa stage. In this stage, which results in an adult butterfly, there is a transformative chemical breakdown and reformation of all but certain thorax structures. The adult butterfly emerges from the pupal case and mates with its own species, and the female completes the cycle by laying her eggs on specific plants.

Abbreviations and Technical Notes

The following abbreviations are used for wing pattern descriptions:

fw = front wing

hw = hind wing

upf = upper front wing

uph = upper hind wing

unf = under front wing

unh = under hind wing

ups = both upper

Viewing and Photographing

There are many cameras that are suitable for photographing butterflies. Bob uses a Nikon N90 body with a hand-held SB 25 flash, and a Nikon 105 mm 1:1 macro lens with auto-focus, set at f16 or f22 for maximum depth of field. Priscilla likes the new, light Nikon N80 with a compact SB 15 flash unit, and she also uses the 105 mm Nikon macro lens but prefers to focus it manually. She prefers Fuji Sensia II for its natural color. All their photos are taken of live butterflies under natural conditions.

Close-focus binoculars are most necessary for observing butterflies. With today's technology, it is possible to find many models that focus closer than six feet. There is a wide range of quality, weight, size and price. The Brodkins both use the Bausch and Lomb 8x42 Elite, a very fine glass that they use for birding also. We have dealt with Eagle Optics, 800-289-1132, for many years. They are willing to take the time to discuss your needs and, if you ask, they will test your glass before shipping.

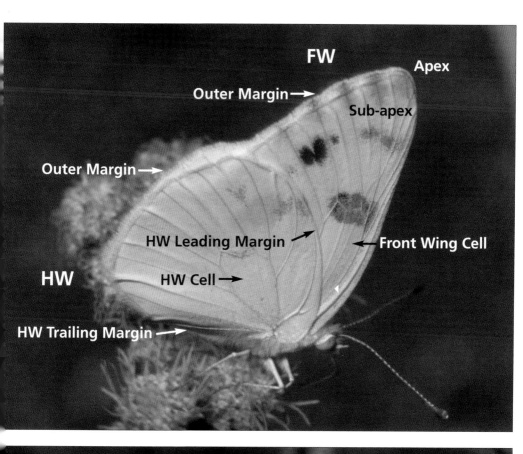

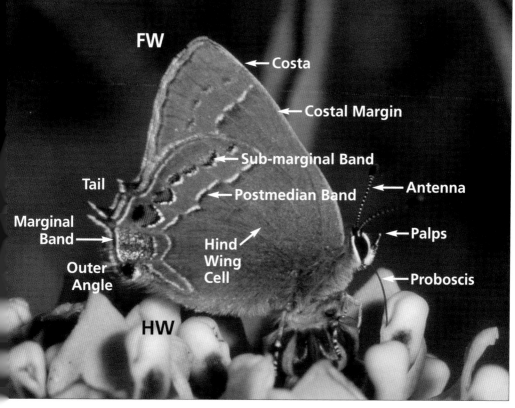

Butterfly Gardening

There is no doubt that there are fewer individual butterflies today than 100 or even 50 years ago. Gardening for butterflies could remedy that decline, at least in part. Gardening for butterflies also creates habitat for many other insects, spiders, birds and lizards. The difference from formal or vegetable gardening in gardening for butterflies is the selection of nectar and host plants that will attract and produce butterflies. Add a few nectar plants such as Butterfly Mist (*Ageratum corybosum*), milkweeds (*Asclepius* species), Trailing Lantana (*Lantana montevidensis*), *Tithonia* and Butterfly Bush (*Buddleia* species) to your garden, and you will be amazed at the number of butterflies that stop by. You will learn quite a bit about butterfly behavior by watching them in your own garden. Many of the photographs in this book were taken in our back yards.

If you want learn more, we suggest that you start with a pamphlet called *Desert Butterfly Gardening* published by the Arizona Native Plant Society, P.O. Box 41206, Sun Station, Tucson AZ 85717. Visit a public butterfly garden, or start your own.

Selected public butterfly gardens in southeastern Arizona:

Patagonia Butterfly Garden

Tucson Botanical Gardens, 2150 N. Alvernon Road, Tucson

Arizona-Sonora Desert Museum, Kinney Road, Tucson

Bisbee—at the base of Brewery Gulch.

Organizations:

The North American Butterfly Association (NABA)—4 Delaware Road, Morristown, NJ 07960; (973) 285-0907; www.naba.org—is a non-profit organization devoted to the non-consumptive study, appreciation and conservation of butterflies. There is one NABA chapter in Arizona, the Southeast Arizona Butterfly Association (SEABA)—P.O Box 1012, Hereford AZ 85615; www.naba.org/chapters/nabasa/home.html. It has monthly meetings, field trips and other activities.

The Lepidopterists' Society is another non-profit organization open to all who are interested in butterflies and moths. For information contact Kelly Richers, 9417 Carvalho Court, Bakersfield CA; www.furman.edu/~snyder/snyder/lep/.

Butterfly Species

✦

Swallowtails ♦ Family Papilionidae

The unique attributes of Swallowtails are large size and tails in most species. The tails are part of a practical deception that allows individuals to fool predators and live to old age (2–3 weeks). Look at any of the photographs that show the spread upper wings, and ask yourself this question: if you were a predator, which end of the Swallowtail would be the most attractive? The rear end looks like a head end, the tails resemble antennae, and the brilliantly colored eyespots—which often have dark pupils—resemble eyes. Also note that all the lines or spot bands lead a predator's eye toward the rear. Iridescent blue scales add to the overwhelming guise. This is a very serious adaptation that Swallowtails have evolved, and to watch it work with an intelligent bird such as a Steller's Jay is marvelous. The jay, swooping down on a **Western Tiger Swallowtail**, makes a direct strike on an eyespot and tail, and then, a fraction of a second later, the jay drops the partial wing section wondering what happened. The butterfly, of course, has quickly flown away with no harm done to its vital essence—which is to mate and lay eggs.

In certain species of Swallowtails (**Black**, **Baird's**, **Anise** and **Indra**), the males fly to hilltops to await virgin females. Unmated females apparently know to come up out of valleys to find virile males. In other species, the males patrol with a rapid flight from a few yards off the ground in search of females. Once mating has begun, the pair stays clasped together for several hours, and if they are disturbed it is the female who flies with the male in tow.

The first larval stages often look like bird droppings to avoid predation, but a larva in later stages develops prominent fake eyespots, which along with a protrudable forked gland (**ostmeterium: 329d**) make it resemble a snake. In most species the pupae hibernate. During drought years in Arizona, pupae can stay in this stage for more than one year waiting for a better chance to find nectar and host plant abundance.

Of the 24 species of Swallowtail that occur in the United States, 13 have been found in Arizona.

Black Swallowtail male, *Papilio polyxenes asterius* **9**

Swallowtails ◆ Subfamily Papilioninae

Black Swallowtail ◆ *Papilio polyxenes* 9; 11a, b

KEY FIELD MARKS: Male *ups* has 2 rows of yellow spots (9); female *ups* has one row of yellow spots (11a); *unh* has two rows of seven orange spots with an extra orange spot just forward of the median spot row (sometimes absent); abdomen black with 2 rows of yellow spots (11b); tegula black; eyespot pupil centered (9 and 11b).

SIZE: $2^5/_8$–4 inches

ADULTS FLY: 11 February to 3 November in southeastern Arizona

HOST PLANTS: dill, celery, parsnips, umbels and turpentine-broom (in western desert)

RANGE: throughout Arizona except the extreme southwest (Yuma and La Paz Counties) (Also: CA, NV, UT, CO, NM)

HABITAT: lower mountain areas, desert

SIMILAR SPECIES: Baird's (page 12): tegula yellow, *unh* yellow spots, eyespot pupil not centered. Indra (page 12): abdomen all black (mostly), *unh* yellow spots. Anise (page 14): abdomen black with one or two yellow bands. Pipevine (page 22): only one row of orange spots *unh*.

'Baird's' Old World Swallowtail ♦ *Papilio machaon bairdii* 13a

KEY FIELD MARKS: Similar to Black Swallowtail but differs in that (1) Baird's has **tegula yellow** not black; (2) **black pupil** in eyespot is **not centered** but touches the inner edge; and (3) *unh* has mostly **yellow** spots not orange.

SIZE: $2^1/_2$–$3^3/_8$ inches

ADULTS FLY: April through September

HOST PLANTS: **sunflower, parsnip, cow-parsnip**

RANGE: the mountainous northern half of Arizona (Also: CA, NV, UT, CO, NM)

HABITAT: canyons, river valleys, and many types of open habitats

SIMILAR SPECIES: **Black** (page 10): **tegula black,** *unh* orange spots, black pupil in eyespot **centered. Indra: abdomen** mostly black, not with row of yellow spots. **Anise** (page 14): **abdomen** with yellow band(s), not yellow spots on *uns*. **Pipevine** (page 22): **one** row of *unh* spots.

Indra Swallowtail ♦ *Papilio indra* 13b

KEY FIELD MARKS: *unh* has mostly **yellow** spots; **abdomen all black** (or with yellow dash near rear).

SIZE: 2–$2^3/_4$ inches

ADULTS FLY: May through June; July and August—partial brood for *kiababensis*

HOST PLANTS: **parsleys** and **turpentine-broom** (when normal hosts are eaten up)

RANGE: extreme northern Arizona in mountainous areas (Also: CA, NV, UT, CO, NM)

HABITAT: mountainous areas from canyon bottoms to mountain tops

SIMILAR SPECIES: **Black** (page 10): *unh* with orange spots, abdomen black with row of yellow spots. **Baird's: abdomen** black with row of yellow spots. **Anise** (page 14): *unh* no yellow or orange spots, abdomen with **yellow** band(s). **Pipevine** (page 22): **one** row of spots *unh*.

Anise Swallowtail ♦ *Papilio zelicaon* 15a, b

KEY FIELD MARKS: *ups* has **broad yellow band** (**15a**); *uns* **cream-colored** (**15b**); **abdomen** black with one or two yellow longitudinal bands; **eyespot** with **centered pupil**.

SIZE: 2$\frac{1}{4}$–3 Inches

ADULTS FLY: late May to early July

FOOD PLANTS: **celery, chuchupate, parsleys, parsnip, yampa**

RANGE: mountainous northern Arizona (Also: CA, NV, UT, CO, NM)

HABITAT: many types of open areas in mountainous areas

SIMILAR SPECIES: **Black** (page 10): **abdomen** with row of yellow spots, *unh* with orange spots. **Baird's** (page 12): **abdomen** with row of yellow spots, *unh* with yellow spots. **Indra** (page 12): **abdomen** mostly black, *unh* with yellow spots. **Pipevine** (page 22): *unh* **one** row of orange spots.

Western Tiger Swallowtail ♦ *Papilio rutulus* **17a, b**

KEY FIELD MARKS: *upf* wide black vertical stripes (narrow inner stripe continues into *uph*); *unh* post-basal black band with cream color at base (**17b**); **tail** broadly banded with yellow on the inside edge.

SIZE: $2^1/_2$–$3^3/_8$ inches

ADULTS FLY: June and July

HOST PLANTS: **chokecherry, bitter cherry, quaking aspen, narrow-leaf cottonwood, willows,** and **thin-leaf alder**

RANGE: the mountainous north, east and southeast, but not in the desert areas of the south and west (Also: CA, NV, UT, CO, NM)

HABITAT: mountain riparian

SIMILAR SPECIES: **Two-tailed Swallowtail** (page 18): two tails; inside edge of tail **not** heavily edged with yellow

Two-tailed Swallowtail ♦ *Papilio multicaudata* 19a, b

KEY FIELD MARKS: Similar to **Western Tiger Swallowtail** but black *upf* vertical bars **narrower**. **Hind wing** has two tails.

SIZE: $2^3/_4$–$5^1/_4$ inches

ADULTS FLY: the last week of February to the second week of November

HOST PLANTS: **bitter cherry, chokecherry, Arizona rosewood, single-leaf ash, hoptree** and **Arizona sycamore**

RANGE: most of Arizona except in the extreme west and southwest (Also: CA, NV, UT, CO, NM)

HABITAT: lower mountain canyons and slopes, cities

BIOLOGICAL NOTES: This individual has been attacked by a bird. Note the missing eyespots and part of the inner tail on the right side. (See page 8 for discussion.)

SIMILAR SPECIES: **Three-tailed Swallowtail** (page 354) has **three** tails and **one fewer** vertical stripe on *upf*.

Note: As of this writing the Arizona State Legislature has declared the Two-tailed Swallowtail the state butterfly of Arizona.

Giant Swallowtail ♦ *Papilio cresphontes* 21

KEY FIELD MARKS: *ups* two yellow bands meeting on front wing; tails long, spatula-shaped, yellow, with a black border; abdomen yellow with a black dorsal line.

SIZE: $3^1/_2$–$5^5/_8$ inches

ADULTS FLY: mid-March to the third week in November

HOST PLANTS: citrus and hoptree

RANGE: western, central and southeastern Arizona (Also: CA, UT, CO, NM)

HABITAT: lower mountains, cities

Pipevine Swallowtail ♦ *Battus philenor* 23a, b

KEY FIELD MARKS: *uph* **iridescent blue** with **one row** of submarginal spots; *unh* **one row** of roundish orange spots.

SIZE: 2³/₈–4³/₄ inches

ADULTS FLY: mid-January through mid-November

HOST PLANT: **Indian root**

RANGE: Arizona generally below 6,000 feet elevation (Also: CA, NV, UT, CO, NM)

HABITAT: foothills, desert, scrub, gardens

NOTES: The host plant has a chemical, aristolochoic acid, which discourages herbivores. The larva of the **Pipevine Swallowtail**, however, is able to bypass this deterrent, store the acid, and pass it on to the pupa and the adult. Vertebrate predators learn to avoid eating the larva, pupa and adult because of the unpleasant flavor. Because of its abundance, the **Pipevine Swallowtail** serves as the model in a Batesian mimicry complex with the **Black Swallowtail** (see page 10) and the **Red-spotted Admiral** (see page 194). Vertebrate predators do not attack these mimics (recalling their unpleasant experience with the **Pipevine Swallowtail**), even though they possess no unpleasant chemicals. By hovering just inches off the ground, the female **Pipevine Swallowtail** is able to find the cryptic, irregularly triangular leaves of the host plant—first by leaf shape and then by chemistry. Before laying eggs, the female searches for previously laid eggs. If none are found, she lays 1–10 eggs in a cluster on the underside of a leaf.

SIMILAR SPECIES: **Black** (page 10), **Baird's** (page 12) and **Indra** (page 12) have **two** rows of spots on the *unh*.

Whites and Sulphurs ◆ Family Pieridae

The butterflies in this family are small to large; white, yellow, orange, greenish or a combination of these four colors. Because many species have a rapid, 4–5 mph, straight-line flight, they are frustrating to identify, especially for beginning butterfly watchers. Fortunately, when they do nectar or puddle, close study is possible. With a little experience, one can identify most of them when they are flying by their size, unique flight, and coloration. Their wings are closed when perched, so that only the *unh* and part of the *unf* is visible. Nevertheless, enough can be seen with this limited view to identify them.

The larvae of many White species feed on plants in the mustard family, which contain mustard oils. Mustard oils are distasteful to many vertebrate predators, who learn that white-colored butterflies should be avoided. Thus, White species may be part of a Mullerian mimicry complex. It is interesting to note that some females of several species—including **Orange (39)**, **Clouded, Cloudless** and **Large-Orange Sulphurs (47)**—have a white form and are considered Batesian mimics of White species.

Of the 55–60 North American species of Pieridae, 36 have been found in Arizona.

Chiricahua White female **25**

Whites ◆ Subfamily Pierinae

Chiricahua White ◆ *Neophasia terlootii* 25, 27a, b

KEY FIELD MARKS: **Male** *upf* and *unf* wide solid **black triangle along leading edge**, with **two** rows of white spots at **apex** and **sub-apex** (**27a, b**); female pattern similar to that of male but has various hues of **orange** (**25**).

SIZE: 2–2^3/$_8$ inches

ADULTS FLY: mid-June to mid-November, markedly heavier in the fall

HOST PLANTS: **ponderosa** and **Apache pine**

RANGE: the mountains of southeastern Arizona (Also: NM)

HABITAT: pine forests

Pine White ◆ *Neophasia menapia* 27c, d

KEY FIELD MARKS: *upf* and *unf* **narrow black leading edge curves inward** with **one** row of white spots at **apex**.

Size: 1^3/$_4$–2 inches

ADULTS FLY: late July to early September

HOST PLANTS: **ponderosa pine, Colorado pinyon** and **Douglas fir**

RANGE: the mountains of central, central-eastern, and northern Arizona (Also: CA, NV, UT, CO, NM).

HABITAT: pine forests

Spring White ♦ *Pontia sisymbrii* 29a, b

KEY FIELD MARKS: *unh* veins bordered by black; postmedial band of V's pointing backwards to trailing edge (29b); *upf* has a narrow black rectangle near the mid-costa with no white line in the center (29a).

SIZE: 1–1³/₈ inches

ADULTS FLY: late February through June

HOST PLANTS: rock cress, tansy mustards, and lacepod

RANGE: throughout Arizona except the extreme southwest (Also: CA, NV, UT, CO, NM)

HABITAT: desert, lower canyons, chaparral

Checkered White ♦ *Pontia protodice* 29c, d

KEY FIELD MARKS: *upf* large rectangle with white center line at mid-costa (29c); *unh* veins yellowish; submarginal brown zig-zag band forms V's pointing backwards along veins (29d) male *unh* white in fall.

SIZE: 1¹/₂–2 inches

ADULTS FLY: March through October

HOST PLANTS: various mustards including rock cress, black mustard, pepper grass, shepherd's purse, and tansy mustards

RANGE: throughout Arizona (Also: CA, NV, UT, CO, NM)

HABITAT: open areas

SIMILAR SPECIES: Western White *Pontia occidentalis* (not shown): *unh* gray-green along the veins. Becker's White (page 30): U-shaped green on *unh*. Spring White: no white in *upf* rectangle. Mustard White (page 30): *unh* veins bordered by black. Cabbage White (page 30): *upf* apex solid black.

Mustard White ♦ *Pieris napi* 31a

KEY FIELD MARKS: *unh* veins **bordered by black, yellow spot** at costa base; *upf* apex **mostly white.**

SIZE: 1³/₈–1⁵/₈ inches

ADULTS FLY: May through August

HOST PLANTS: mustards including **rock cress, winter cress, black mustard, bitter-cress,** *Draba*, and **radish**

RANGE: the mountains of northern and eastern Arizona (Also: CA, NV, UT, CO, NM)

HABITAT: meadows in conifer forests

SIMILAR SPECIES: see page 28

Cabbage White ♦ *Pieris rapae* 31b

KEY FIELD MARKS: *uns* yellowish; *upf* solid black apex.

SIZE: 1¹/₂–2 inches

ADULTS FLY: all year, weather permitting

HOST PLANTS: various wild and domesticated mustards including **rock cress, black mustard, shepherd's purse, radish,** and **cabbages; bee-plant**

RANGE: throughout Arizona except the extreme southwest (Also: CA, NV, UT, CO, NM)

HABITAT: open areas, cities

SIMILAR SPECIES: see page 28

Becker's White ♦ *Pontia beckerii* 31c

KEY FIELD MARKS: *unh* greenish submarginal band has **U-shaped** pattern.

SIZE: 1³/₈–1³/₄ inches

ADULTS FLY: April through September

HOST PLANTS: various mustards including **desert plume, black mustard, rock cress, pepper grass** and **tansy mustard**

RANGE: extreme northern Arizona (Also: CA, NV, UT, CO, NM)

HABITAT: foothills, high desert

SIMILAR SPECIES: see page 28

Pearly Marble ♦ *Euchloe hyantis* 33

KEY FIELD MARKS: *unh* wide **greenish-yellow bands**—well connected, discrete; white areas **pearly** white.

SIZE: $1^1/_8$–$1^3/_8$ inches

ADULTS FLY: late February to early May

HOST PLANTS: various mustards including **rock cress, squaw cabbage, tansy mustard, pepper grass** and **twist flower**

RANGE: western (excluding the extreme southwest), southern and the Four Corners area of Arizona (Also: CA, NV, UT, CO, NM)

HABITAT: pinyon-juniper, sagebrush, and open areas

Large Marble ♦ *Euchloe ausonides* (no photo)

KEY FIELD MARKS: *uns* very similar to **Pearly Marble**, but white area **not pearly** white.

SIZE: 1–$1^3/_4$ inches

ADULTS FLY: May to early July

HOST PLANTS: mustards including **rock cress, winter cress, black mustard, tansy mustard, radish** and **tumble mustard**

RANGE: extreme northern Arizona (Also: CA, NV, UT, CO, NM)

HABITAT: meadows and river bottoms

Sara Orangetip ♦ *Anthocharis sara* 35a

KEY FIELD MARKS: Male *upf* orange patch below apex **crosses to both margins;** *unh* pattern **not appearing banded** but dispersed.

SIZE: 1–1$\frac{1}{2}$ inches

ADULTS FLY: after the first week in January through April

HOST PLANTS: mustards including **rock cress, winter cress, black mustard, shepherd's purse, tansy mustard** and **radish**

RANGE: throughout most of Arizona in proper habitat (Also: CA, NV, UT, CO, NM)

HABITAT: oak woodland and high desert

'Pima' Desert Orangetip ♦ *Anthocharis cethura pima* 35b, c

KEY FIELD MARKS: Male *upf yellow-orange patch* below apex **does not cross wing** (**35b**); *unh* yellow green pattern appears **banded** (**35c**).

SIZE: 1–1$\frac{1}{2}$ inches

ADULTS FLY: early February to the third week of April

HOST PLANTS: Mustards: **California mustard, tansy mustard** and *Streptanthella*

RANGE: western and southern third of Arizona except for the extreme southwest corner (Also: CA, UT, NM)

HABITAT: desert and foothills

NOTES: Males patrol hilltops and wait for females.

Sulphurs ◆ Subfamily Coliadinae

Orange Sulphur ◆ *Colias eurytheme* 37, 39c

KEY FIELD MARKS: *unh* centerspot—one large and one small; *unf* slight hint of orange showing through; *ups* orange with wide black border; *unh* of female can be white (**39c**).

SIZE: 1$^1/_2$–2$^3/_8$ inches

ADULTS FLY: all year in warmer areas of Arizona

HOST PLANTS: **locoweeds, licorice, Spanish clover, lupines, beans, Colorado River hemp, clovers, vetch** and **alfalfa**

RANGE: throughout Arizona (Also: CA, NV, UT, CO, NM)

HABITAT: wide variety of open habitats

NOTES: Can hybridize with **Clouded Sulphur**. White-form females cannot be distinguished from white-form **Clouded Sulphur** females.

SIMILAR SPECIES: **Clouded Sulphur** (page 40): *ups* yellow. **Southern Dogface** (page 38) has dog face *unf* and pointed *fw* apex.

Southern Dogface ♦ *Colias (Zerene) cesonia* 39a, b, 347a

KEY FIELD MARKS: *uns* with similar circles and spots as **Orange Sulphur**; *unf* black spot is the **"eye" of the dog face** showing through from the *upf*; apex pointed; fall form has pink lines in *unh* (39b).

SIZE: $1^7/_8$–$2^1/_2$ inches

ADULTS FLY: all year, weather permitting

HOST PLANTS: **bastard indigo, alfalfa** and *Dalea* species

RANGE: throughout Arizona (Also: CA, NV, UT, CO, NM)

HABITAT: wide variety of open areas

SIMILAR SPECIES: **Orange Sulphur** (page 36) and **Clouded Sulphur** (page 40) do not have *unf* dog face.

NOTE: This and other Sulphurs rarely hold their wings open except when mating or courting. For a natural look at the opened wings see 347a.

Clouded Sulphur ◆ *Colias philodice* 41a

KEY FIELD MARKS: *ups* all **yellow** with wide black border; *uns* all **yellow**, no orange showing through from *ups*.

SIZE: 1⁵/₈–2¹/₂ inches

ADULTS FLY: the last week in April to the first week in November

HOST PLANTS: **ground plum, alfalfa, clovers, American vetch** and **burclover**

RANGE: northern edge and eastern part of Arizona; the Gila River Valley (Also: CA, NV, UT, CO, NM)

HABITAT: wide variety of open habitats

SIMILAR SPECIES: **Orange Sulphur** (page 36): orange *ups* but some individuals cannot be separated in the field. **Southern Dogface** (page 38): has dogface on *unf* and pointed *fw* apex.

Queen Alexandra's Sulphur ◆ *Colias alexandra* 41b

KEY FIELD MARKS: *unh* greenish with **vague white spot in center**; *unf* yellow with **greenish** apex.

SIZE: 1¹/₂–2 inches

ADULTS FLY: May through August

HOST PLANTS: **locoweeds, sweet vetch, Alfalfa, purple loco, golden pea, clover, American vetch**

RANGE: north and central eastern Arizona (Also CA, NV, UT, CO, NM)

HABITAT: mountain meadows

SIMILAR SPECIES: **Lyside Sulphur** (page 40): no overlap in range; vertical bar center *unh*; yellow only at base *unf*.

Lyside Sulphur ◆ *Kricogonia lyside* 41c, d

KEY FIELD MARKS: *uns* whitish or greenish with **yellow** at *unf* **base**; *unh* a **vague darker bar** perpendicular to veins

SIZE: 1¹/₄–2 inches

ADULTS FLY: yearly monsoon influx species—second week in July through third week in November

HOST PLANT: not known in Arizona

RANGE: extreme southern Arizona (Also: CA, CO, NV)

HABITAT: dry scrub

SIMILAR SPECIES: **Queen Alexander Sulphur**: yellow in *unf* extensive, vague white spot *unh*.

White Angled-sulphur ♦ *Anteos clorinde* 43a

KEY FIELD MARKS: *uns* large greenish angle-edged wing; *unh* **center spot roundish** with thick vein **above and below** the center spot; *ups* white.

SIZE: 2³/₄–3¹/₂ inches

ADULTS FLY: regular monsoon influx species—mid-July to mid-November

HOST PLANTS: not known in Arizona

RANGE: southeastern Arizona (Also: UT, CO)

SIMILAR SPECIES: **Yellow Angled-sulphur**: yellow *ups*, elongated *unh* center spot with thick vein above spot only. From other large sulphurs by angled wing edges.

Yellow Angled-sulphur ♦ *Anteos maerula* 43b

KEY FIELD MARKS: *uns* large greenish-yellow angle-edged wing; *unh* **center spot elongated** (not circular) with thick vein only above this spot; *ups* yellow.

SIZE: 3–3¹/₂ inches

ADULTS FLY: rare monsoon influx species—mid-August to the beginning of November

HOST PLANTS: not known in Arizona

RANGE: extreme southeastern Arizona (Also: NM)

SIMILAR SPECIES: **White Angled-sulphur**: white *ups*; center *unh* spot round with thick vein above and below this spot.

Cloudless Sulphur ♦ *Phoebis sennae* 45a, b

KEY FIELD MARKS: Male (**45a**) large, **all-yellow wings** both *ups* and *uns*; spots on *uns* small and vague; female (**45b**) *unh* **two spots** large and **subequal**; *unf* many upper center spots **band of spots from apex offset.**

SIZE: $1^7/_8$–$2^1/_2$

ADULTS FLY: late March through early January, weather pemitting

HOST PLANTS: many species of *Senna*

RANGE: throughout Arizona (Also: CA, NV, UT, CO, NM)

HABITAT: wide variety of open spaces

SIMILAR SPECIES: Male **Large Orange Sulphur** (page 46) has orange *ups*; female **Large Orange Sulphur** has *unf* band continuous.

Large Orange Sulphur ♦ *Phoebis agarithe* 47a, b

KEY FIELD MARKS: Male (**47a**) similar to **Cloudless Sulphur** except **orange** *ups*; female (**47b**) similar to **Cloudless Sulphur** except **band from** *unf* **apex continuous** (not offset); female white form **49a**.

SIZE: 2–3 inches

ADULTS FLY: records from April through early November, but mainly a regular monsoon influx species from mid-June

HOST PLANT: **feather bush**

RANGE: southern half of Arizona (Also: CA, CO, NM)

HABITAT: wide variety of open areas

SIMILAR SPECIES: **Cloudless Sulphur** (page 44)

Orange-barred Sulphur ♦ *Phoebis philea* 49b

KEY FIELD MARKS: Male a large yellow sulphur with an **orange bar** on mid-costa of *upf* and **wide orange edge** to *uph*; female (**49b**) similar to **Cloudless** and **Large Orange Sulphur** except *uns* **suffused with orange**.

SIZE: 2¹/₄–3³/₈ inches

ADULTS FLY: a rare monsoon influx straggler (occasionally breeds) between the end of July to the beginning of October

HOST PLANT: *Senna*

RANGE: southeastern Arizona (Also: CA, NV, CO, NM)

SIMILAR SPECIES: **Cloudless Sulphur** (page 44) and **Large Orange Sulphur** (page 46) do not have orange bars on *upf* or suffusion of orange on *unh*.

Boisduval's Yellow ♦ *Eurema boisduvaliana* **51a**

KEY FIELD MARKS: A **tailed** yellow similar to **Mexican Yellow**; *uns* pinkish-beige apex; *unh* diagonal line is pinkish-beige and usually **wider** than in **Mexican Yellow**.

SIZE: $1^1/_4$–$1^1/_2$ inches

ADULTS FLY: late March to late November—a regular influx species that occasionally breeds

HOST PLANT: *Senna*

RANGE: extreme southeastern Arizona (Also: CA, NV, CO, NM)

HABITAT: open woodland

SIMILAR SPECIES: **Mexican Yellow** shows white on *unf* and faint brownish diagonal on *unh*.

Mexican Yellow ♦ *Eurema mexicana* **51b**

KEY FIELD MARKS: A **tailed** yellow; *unf* shows **white** below apex but can have a pinkish beige color; *unh* **faint diagonal line** from sub apex; *ups* yellow.

SIZE: $1^1/_4$–$2^1/_4$ inches

ADULTS FLY: all year, weather permitting

HOST PLANTS: **New Mexican locust** and **whiteball acacia**

RANGE: throughout Arizona (Also: NM)

SIMILAR SPECIES: **Boisduval's Yellow** has less white showing on *unf*, pinkish-beige *unf* apex, and pinkish-beige diagonal on *unf*.

Tailed Orange ♦ *Eurema proterpia* **51c, d**

KEY FIELD MARKS: Wet season form (**51c**) has no tail; *unh* has **no spots**—veins slightly lighter than ground color; dry season form (**51d**) *hw* is tailed, *unh* with many vague darker spots, *ups* bright orange.

SIZE:$1^1/_4$–$1^3/_4$ inches

ADULTS FLY: mid-July through first week in January, weather permitting

HOST PLANT: *Senna chamaecrista*

RANGE: central and southeastern Arizona (Also: NM)

HABITAT: open woodland

SIMILAR SPECIES: Wet season form of **Sleepy Orange** (page 56) has *unh* marks.

Little Yellow ♦ *Eurema lisa* 53a

KEY FIELD MARKS: a small Yellow; *unh* two black center dots and **two black basal dots**.

SIZE: 1–1^1/$_2$ inches

ADULTS FLY: late April to mid-May; early July through October—an uncommon influx species, but possibly breeds occasionally

HOST PLANTS: not known in Arizona, but in other places uses species of *Senna*

RANGE: southeastern Arizona along the Mexican border

HABITAT: open areas and riparian

SIMILAR SPECIES: **Dina Yellow** (page 54) has three black dots *unh*. **Mimosa Yellow** lacks the two black dots at base of *unh*.

Mimosa Yellow ♦ *Eurema nise* 53b, c

KEY FIELD MARKS: a small Yellow; very similar to **Little Yellow** but **lacks the two black basal dots** *unh*; female (**53b**) has **pinkish-brown** at *unh* apex; winter form light brown **uns**. male **53c**.

SIZE: 1–1^1/$_4$ inches

ADULTS FLY: mid-April to the third week in June and mid-August to mid-September. An irregular influx species that possibly breeds occasionally.

HOST PLANTS: not known in Arizona, but uses **whitethorn acacia** in Sonora

RANGE: southeastern Arizona along the Mexican border (Also: CA, NV, UT, CO, NM)

HABITAT: open areas and riparian

SIMILAR SPECIES: **Dina Yellow** (page 54) has three black dots *unh*. **Little Yellow** has two black dots at base of **unh**.

Dina Yellow ♦ *Eurema dina* 55a, b

KEY FIELD MARKS: Male *unh* no pinkish brown at apex; two black dots in center and one forward; female *unh* similar to male except pinkish-brown at apex.

SIZE: $1^1/_2$–$1^7/_8$ inches

ADULTS FLY: irregular moonsoon influx species August through mid-September

HOST PLANTS: not known in Arizona

RANGE: southeastern Arizona

HABITAT: open areas and riparian

SIMILAR SPECIES: **Little Yellow** (page 52) has two black dots at at base of *unh*. **Mimosa Yellow** (page 52) has only two dots in center of *unh*.

Barred Yellow ♦ *Eurema daira* 55c, d

KEY FIELD MARKS: *unh* creamy white or with many very tiny spots; winter form (**55d**) browner; male *ups* has black bar on lower margin of *fw*.

SIZE: 1–$1^3/_8$ inches

ADULTS FLY: an uncommon monsoon influx species from early August to mid-October

HOST PLANTS: not known in Arizona

RANGE: extreme southeastern Arizona

HABITAT: mid-elevation hilly areas

SIMILAR SPECIES: Dainty Sulphur (page 56): gray on *unh*. **Mimosa** (page 52). **Little** (page 52) and **Dina Yellow** show yellow at *unh* costa.

Dainty Sulphur ♦ *Nathalis iole* 57a

KEY FIELD MARKS: Tiny—the smallest Sulphur; winter form *unf* greenish apex, **yellow-orange base**; *unh* **greenish** with cream-colored postmedian costal bar; wet-season form *uns* more yellow (not shown).

SIZE: $7/8$–1 inch

ADULTS FLY: all year, weather permitting

HOST PLANTS: **dogweed, common beggar's tick, sneeze weed, cosmos, Spanish needles** and Hopi tea greenthread

RANGE: throughout Arizona (Also: CA, NV, UT, CO, NM)

HABITAT: a wide variety of open areas

Sleepy Orange ♦ *Eurema nicippe* 57b, c

KEY FIELD MARKS: *ups* similar to **Tailed Orange** but *hw* has black outer edge and has no tail; *unh* orange-yellow—has **two vague median spots** on the top edge and the bottom edge and an **additional diagonal line towards outer edge**; winter form (57c) brown *uns*.

SIZE: $1 1/2$–2 inches

ADULTS FLY: all year, weather permitting

HOST PLANTS: several species of *Senna*

HABITAT: a wide variety of open habitats and forest

RANGE: throughout Arizona (Also: CA, NV, UT, CO, NM)

Gossamer-wing Butterflies ♦ Family Lycaenidae

The family of little butterflies (Lycaenidae) includes Hairstreaks, Blues, Coppers and Harvesters (not found in Arizona). The Hairstreaks are so named because many have flimsy hair-like "tails" on the hind wing edge (but many do not have obvious tails, while some Blues and Coppers do!). The upper wings are sometimes brilliant iridescent blue (some are coppery or brown), but for the butterfly watcher this is only supplemental information, because the Hairstreaks rarely open their wings while perched. To appreciate the unique under wing patterning of this group of species, one must follow the flying individual with its incredibly erratic flight until it lands. On the ground or on a flower it is stationary, which increases its vulnerability to predators. The Hairstreaks have adapted to this vulnerability by appearing to have a "head end" at the rear. Predators will bite the "false head" at the rear and miss the body. This is similar to the deception of the Swallowtails discussed earlier. The following five features provide the deception: 1) brightly colored spots (orange or blue or both) resembling eyes at the corner of the hind wing; 2) hind wing "tails" to represent the palps and antennae; 3) flaring of the hind wing corner to resemble a head; 4) bands on the under wings all leading one's eye to the false head; and 5) rubbing hind wings back and forth to draw attention to the false head. For good examples of these characteristics see pages 59 and 61.

Most larvae of Lycaenidae have interesting mutualistic relationships with ants (see page 82).

Hairstreaks ♦ Subfamily Theclinae

Gray Hairstreak ♦ *Strymon melinus* 59

KEY FIELD MARKS: *unh* with a **blue spot bordered on either side by orange spots**, and a postmedian band bordered inwardly with **black and orange**.

SIZE: $^7/_8$–1$^1/_8$ inches

ADULTS FLY: all year, weather permitting

HOST PLANTS: many families (pea, mallow, buckthorn, buckwheat, etc.)

RANGE: throughout Arizona (Also: CA, NV, UT, CO, NM)

HABITAT: a wide variety of open areas

SIMILAR SPECIES: **Colorado Hairstreak** (page 62), **Soapberry Hairstreak** (page 60) and **Leda Ministreak** have lines inwardly from *unh* postmedian band.

NOTES: Uses at least 24 species of host plant in Arizona.

Soapberry Hairstreak ♦ *Phaeostrymon alcestis* 61a

KEY FIELD MARKS: *unh* with a blue spot between two orange spots and then a few more **submarginal orange spots above** a postmedian white band bordered inwardly with black and a **short median white band.**

SIZE: 1–1^1/$_4$ inches

ADULTS FLY: mid-May to mid-June

HOST PLANT: **soapberry**

RANGE: central to southeastern Arizona where host plant occurs (Also: CO, NM)

HABITAT: washes in middle elevations

SIMILAR SPECIES: **Leda Ministreak:** inner *unh* line **orange (not white); lacks** row of orange spots. **Gray Hairstreak lacks** inner *unh* line. **Colorado Hairstreak** has **iridescent blue** *unh* margin.

Leda Ministreak ♦ *Ministrymon leda* 61b, c

KEY FIELD MARKS: *unh* with blue spot between two orange spots, a postmedian band bordered inwardly with orange, and **short inner orange bands;** *unf* short inner orange bands (from postmedian band). Fall form similar pattern but **wide light gray area outward from postmedian band to margin**; orange colors much **reduced.**

SIZE: ^{5}/$_8$–^{7}/$_8$ inch

ADULTS FLY: early April to mid-December

HOST PLANT: **velvet mesquite**

RANGE: throughout except north-central Arizona (Also: CA, NV, UT, CO, NM)

HABITAT: desert, mesquite forests, open areas

SIMILAR SPECIES: **Soapberry Hairstreak: more orange spots in** *unh* submarginal band; short white median band. **Gray Hairstreak** (page 58) **lacks short inner line** on *unh*. **Colorado Hairstreak** (page 62) has iridescent marginal band.

Arizona Hairstreak ♦ *Erora quaderna* 63a, b

KEY FIELD MARKS: *unh* green with **orange marginal band** and **two rows of orange dots**; *unf* green with orange band on costa and trailing edge (**63a**); *ups* **iridescent purplish-blue** with cream marginal bands (**63b**).

SIZE: $^7/_8$–1 inch

ADULTS FLY: early March to mid-May and July to mid-August (two broods)

HOST PLANTS: **Fendlers ceanothus** and **white oak**

RANGE: central to southeastern Arizona (Also: NM)

HABITAT: dense oak woodland

Colorado Hairstreak ♦ *Hypaurotis crysalus* 63c

KEY FIELD MARKS: *unh* **iridescent blue marginal band**, two white postmedial bands, with three short bands inward.

SIZE: $1^1/_8$–$1^3/_4$ inches

ADULTS FLY: May to late October

HOST PLANT: **Gambel oak**

RANGE: highlands from the northwest through the central part of Arizona to the southeast (Also: NV, CO, UT, NM)

HABITAT: in and near groves of **Gambel oak**

SIMILAR SPECIES: **Gray Hairstreak** (page 58), **Soapberry Hairstreak** (page 60), and **Leda Ministreak** (page 60) **lack** iridescent blue marginal band.

Silver-banded Hairstreak ◆ *Chlorostrymon simaethis* 65a

KEY FIELD MARKS: *unh* green with wide brown marginal band and postmedian silver band.

SIZE: $7/8$–1 inch

ADULTS FLY: late March to late June and late October to mid-November (two broods)

HOST PLANTS: not known in Arizona

RANGE: western and southern Arizona (Also: CA, NV, UT)

HABITAT: open areas, desert and scrub

SIMILAR SPECIES: Xami Hairstreak: *unh* postmedian band connects to submarginal band three times and ground color is brownish-yellow.

Xami Hairstreak ◆ *Callophrys xami* 65b

KEY FIELD MARKS: *unh* brownish-yellow; postmedian silver band with three forks connecting to the silvery submarginal band.

SIZE: 1–$1^1/8$ inches

ADULTS FLY: March to November

HOST PLANTS: *Graptopetalum*

RANGE: central and southeastern Arizona (Also: CO)

HABITAT: open areas of rocky oak or pine forest

SIMILAR SPECIES: Silver-banded Hairstreak: *unh* postmedian band connects with submarginal band once and ground color is green.

Desert Elfin ◆ *Callophrys fotis* 65c

KEY FIELD MARKS: *unh* tailless with a wide, undulating postmedian band.

SIZE: $3/4$–$7/8$ inch

ADULTS FLY: April through May

HOST PLANT: quinine bush

RANGE: northern and northeastern Arizona (Also: CA, NV, UT, CO, NM)

HABITAT: rocky areas in dry foothills

Western Pine Elfin ♦ *Callophrys eryphon* 67a

KEY FIELD MARKS: *unh* with submarginal **dark zig-zag protruding into the pinkish postmedian band**; tail **very** small.

SIZE: $^7/_8$ inch

ADULTS FLY: June to mid-July

HOST PLANTS: **ponderosa** and **limber pines**; **Douglas fir**

RANGE: northwest corner diagonally to southeast corner of Arizona (Also: CA, NV, UT, CO, NM)

HABITAT: Pine forests

Golden Hairstreak ♦ *Habrodais grunus* 67b

KEY FIELD MARKS: *unh* light brownish with **silvery submarginal lines** at the corner and a darker brown postmedial band; *ups* brown.

SIZE: 1–1$^1/_4$ inches

ADULTS FLY: late June through early August

HOST PLANTS: **oaks**

RANGE: along the Mogollon Rim of central Arizona and Mt. Graham (Also: CA, NV)

HABITAT: Oaks

SIMILAR SPECIES: **Brown Elfin lacks** a tail.

Brown Elfin ♦ *Callophrys augustinus* 67c

KEY FIELD MARKS: *unh* tailless **orangish-brown**; *unf* light tan; *ups* brown.

SIZE: $^3/_4$–$^7/_8$ inch

ADULTS FLY: January through May, weather permitting

HOST PLANTS: **manzanita** and **deerbrush**

RANGE: central, eastern and southeastern Arizona (Also: CA, NV, UT, CO, NM)

HABITAT: mountains, scrub, oak woodland

Ilavia Hairstreak ♦ *Satyrium ilavia* 69a

KEY FIELD MARKS: *unh* brown with blue spot between two orange spots at corner and white postmedial band edged inwardly with black; *unf* orangish costa.

SIZE: $^7/_8$–1 inch

ADULTS FLY: June

HOST PLANT: scrub oak

RANGE: central to southeast Arizona (Also NM)

HABITAT: scrub oak thickets in mid-elevation chaparral

SIMILAR SPECIES: Hedgerow Hairstreak (page 70) lacks orange spots on either side of blue in *unh* corner.

Behr's Hairstreak ♦ *Satyrium behrii* 69b

KEY FIELD MARKS: *unh* tailless with faint larger blue spot under two black spots, the inner bordered outwardly with faint orange; postmedial band undulating white bordered inwardly with black; *ups* orange with dark brown border.

SIZE: 1–1$^1/_8$ inches

ADULTS FLY: July

HOST PLANT: bitter brush

RANGE: northern Arizona (Also: CA, NV, UT, CO, NM)

HABITAT: scrub, arid flats with host plant

SIMILAR SPECIES: Mallow Scrub-Hairstreak (no overlap in range) has two rows of white crescents in the outer edge of *unh*; the inner black spots are roundish.

Mallow Scrub-Hairstreak ♦ *Strymon istapa* 69c

KEY FIELD MARKS: *unh* tailless, postmedial band dark-edged outwardly with white, and two roundish spots inward near base.

SIZE: $^3/_4$–1 inch

ADULTS FLY: late March to early June; early August to November (multiple broods)

HOST PLANTS: alkali mallow

RANGE: across southern Arizona (Also: CA, NV)

HABITAT: desert scrub, open areas

SIMILAR SPECIES: Behr's Hairstreak has orange *ups*, lacks roundish inner *unh* spots, and has inner white dots on *unf*.

Coral Hairstreak ◆ *Satyrium titus* 71a

KEY FIELD MARKS: *unh* large submarginal **coral-colored spots** with a row of postmedian black spots bordered by white.

SIZE: $7/8$–$1 1/4$ inches

ADULTS FLY: July through August

HOST PLANT: **common chokecherry**

RANGE: extreme northeastern Arizona (Also: CA, NV, UT, CO, NM)

HABITAT: open brushy areas

Hedgerow Hairstreak ◆ *Satyrium saepium* 71b

KEY FIELD MARKS: *unh* with **large blue spot at corner**, postmedial band white with black border inwardly, **faint pale vertical line inward**; *ups* coppery.

SIZE: $7/8$–$1 1/8$ inches

ADULTS FLY: late May to early September

HOST PLANTS: **Fendler** and **Gregg ceanothus**

RANGE: northern and central Arizona (Also: CA, NV, UT, CO)

HABITAT: scrub, mountain forests

SIMILAR SPECIES: **Ilavia Hairstreak** (page 68) has **orange spots** in *unh* corner.

Sylvan Hairstreak ◆ *Satyrium sylvinus* 71c

KEY FIELD MARKS: *unh* with **blue spot** bordered above by an **orange spot**; **black spots surrounded by white** forms the postmedian band, short line inward; *ups* **brown** with gray spot near mid-costa on **fw** and faint orange band at corner *hw*.

SIZE: $7/8$–$1 1/8$ inches

ADULTS FLY: mid-July to mid-August

HOST PLANTS: **sandbar** and **arroyo willow**

RANGE: central and central-eastern Arizona (Also: CA, NV, UT, CO, NM)

HABITAT: wet valleys and streamsides

SIMILAR SPECIES: **Ilavia** (page 68) and **Hedgerow Hairstreaks**: *unh* postmedial band not made up of black dots.

'Siva' Juniper Hairstreak ♦ *Callophrys gryneus siva* 73a

KEY FIELD MARKS: *unh* green, a continuous connected **white postmedial band** bordered by **orange**; wide **gray** marginal band; *unf* **brown** with tinges of green; *ups* brown.

SIZE: 1 inch

ADULTS FLY: late February to mid-November

HOST PLANTS: **common** and **alligator juniper**

RANGE: throughout except southwestern Arizona (Also: CA, NV, UT, CO, NM)

HABITAT: juniper and pinyon-juniper woodland

SIMILAR SPECIES: **'Desert' Sheridan's Green** does not have brown in *unf* and **lack** tails. **Xami Hairstreak** (page 64) *unh* has **straight** postmedian band.

'Canyon' Bramble Hairstreak ♦ *Callophrys dumetorum apama* 73b

KEY FIELD MARKS: *unh* tailless with **narrow** white postmedial band bordered inwardly with black and **orange**.

SIZE: 3/4–1 1/8 inches

ADULTS FLY: June through July

HOST PLANTS: **Eriogonum** species

RANGE: north-central through northeastern and down eastern third of Arizona (Also: CA, NV, UT, CO, NM)

HABITAT: foothills

SIMILAR SPECIES: **'Desert' Sheridan's Hairstreak** has a more prominent postmedial band and a **black marginal band**. **"Siva" Juniper Hairstreak** has a wider, whiter postmedial band and a wide silvery marginal band.

'Desert' Sheridan's Hairstreak ♦ *Callophrys sheridanii comstocki* 73c

KEY FIELD MARKS: *unh* tailless, green with white postmedial band bordered inwardly with black; **narrow black marginal band**.

SIZE: 3/4–1 inch

ADULTS FLY: mid-June through July

HOST PLANT: **buckwheat**

RANGE: extreme northwestern through extreme north-central Arizona (Also: CA, NV, UT, CO)

HABITAT: dry open areas near host plant

SIMILAR SPECIES: **Bramble Hairstreak** has narrower postmedial band bordered by **orange**.

Great Purple Hairstreak ♦ *Atlides halesus* 75a

KEY FIELD MARKS: *uns* **three red blotches at base**, iridescent green and blue spots at corner; abdomen **blue and orange**.

SIZE: 1–1³/₄ inches

ADULTS FLY: late February to mid-November

HOST PLANTS: several **mistletoe** species

RANGE: throughout Arizona (Also: CA, NV, UT, CO, NM)

HABITAT: oak, pine-juniper-oak, and riparian woodlands

Thicket Hairstreak ♦ *Callophrys spinetorum* 75b

KEY FIELD MARKS: *unh* with a connected white postmedial band bordered inwardly with black, a faint short vertical line inward, a **submarginal band of gray spots above faint orange and blue spots** at the corner; *ups* steel gray.

SIZE: ⁷/₈–1 inch

ADULTS FLY: late March to late July

HOST PLANTS: **pine mistletoe**

RANGE: mountains throughout Arizona except for the southwest (Also: CA, NV, UT, CO, NM)

HABITAT: coniferous forest

Creamy Stripe-streak ♦ *Arawacus jada* 75c, d

KEY FIELD MARKS: *uns* very pale **tan and cream stripes** with **pale orange spot at** *hw* corner; *ups* blue base with brown upper wings, orange spot at *hw* corner.

SIZE: 1 inch

ADULTS FLY: mid-March to November—a rare stray but may possibly breed

HOST PLANTS: not known in Arizona

RANGE: south-central to southeastern Arizona

HABITAT: open areas near streams

Blues ♦ Subfamily Polyommatinae

Blues are similar to some of the Hairstreaks in that they have bright blue upper-wings, especially the males. Their flight is not as fast and erratic as the Hairstreaks'. It is common to find groups of Blues congregating where there is moist sand or mud. At these so-called puddling parties only males can be found. Apparently these males need certain dissolved salts, amino acids and minerals. They imbibe the necessary elements with their proboscis. They do this on rotting fruits, plant sap, dead animals and dung from mammals (and even ant dung!). The senior author once watched about 50 Blues, Skippers and Brushfoots working on a pile of fresh bobcat scat. Among the concentrated butterflies were competing Dung Beetles collecting little balls of scat to roll away and bury (after depositing their eggs). Although Blues, Skippers, Sulphurs and Swallowtails are the usual components of the puddling party, Brushfoots, Whites and Metalmarks will also join in. When disturbed, the Blues will all appear very similar, flashing their blue upper wings. In a few moments they will land, abruptly closing their wings. The unique pattern of spots on the under wing is the key to distinguishing the species. Can you find and identify the three species of Blues in this photograph?

Each species utilizes a unique set of host plants. The most commonly used are in the pea family, but the buckwheat, rose and saltbush families are also selected. Each species has a unique hibernation stage, but taken as a group they can hibernate as either an egg, larva or pupa. Blues also have close relationships with ants (see page 82).

Western Pygmy-Blue ♦ *Brephidium exile* 79a, b

KEY FIELD MARKS: *uns* orangish with **white dashes** and six or seven **iridescent** unh marginal spots (**79a**); *ups* brownish-orange with dark borders (**79b**).

SIZE: $1/2$–$3/4$ inch

ADULTS FLY: all year, weather permitting

HOST PLANTS: various species of **saltbush; goosefoot, sea purslane** and **Russian thistle**

RANGE: throughout Arizona (Also: CA, NV, UT, CO, NM)

HABITAT: dry open areas

NOTE: This is the smallest North American butterfly.

Spring Azure ♦ *Celastrina ladon* 79 c, d

KEY FIELD MARKS: *uns* (**79c**) **submarginal row of V's pointing** toward the body on both wings, black spots fainter than on most Blues; female *ups* (**79d**) blue with **wide black margin** on the trailing edge and along the upper costa.

SIZE: $7/8$–$1 1/4$ inches

ADULTS FLY: all year, weather permitting

HOST PLANTS: **fern bush, rock spiraea, chokecherry**

RANGE: throughout Arizona except extreme southwest (Also: CA, NV, UT, CO, NM)

HABITAT: open woodland, near moist spots

Ceraunus Blue ♦ *Hemiargus ceraunus* 81a

KEY FIELD MARKS: *unh* with **two black spots** surrounded by white **along costa**, a fainter third black spot lies directly below the inner costa spot (to form a triangle).

SIZE: $5/8$–$7/8$ inch

ADULTS FLY: all year, weather permitting

HOST PLANTS: **whiteball acacia, loco weed, alfalfa, honey mesquite, screwbean mesquite**

RANGE: throughout Arizona except the northeast (Also: CA, NV, UT, CO, NM)

HABITAT: open areas, desert scrub

SIMILAR SPECIES: **Marine** and **Reakirt's Blues** (page 82) both have iridescent spots similar to those of **Ceraunus Blue** on the rear *unh*, but **Reakirt's Blue** has black *unf* spots surrounded by white, and **Marine Blue** has *uns* brown and white bands.

Marine Blue ♦ *Leptotes marina* 81b

KEY FIELD MARKS: *uns* **banded** with white and brown.

SIZE: $3/4$–1 inch

ADULTS FLY: all year, weather permitting

HOST PLANTS: **mesquite, false indigo, catclaw acacia, wild licorice**

RANGE: throughout Arizona (Also: CA, NV, UT, CO, NM)

HABITAT: mesquite woodland and open areas

SIMILAR SPECIES: See **Ceraunus Blue**.

Reakirt's Blue ♦ *Hemiargus isola* 83

KEY FIELD MARKS: *unf* with prominent **postmedial black spots surrounded with white**.

SIZE: $5/8$–1 inch

ADULTS FLY: all year, weather permitting

HOST PLANTS: **whitethorn acacia, mesquite, sweetclovers** and other plants in the pea family

RANGE: throughout Arizona (Also: CA, NV, UT, CO, NM)

HABITAT: thorn scrub, desert, open areas

SIMILAR SPECIES: See **Ceraunus Blue** (page 80).

NOTE: Although it is well known that most Lycaenid and Riodonid butterfly larvae have associations with ants, Diane Wagner, working in southeast Arizona, has provided the first detailed study for a North American species. **Reakirt's Blue** larvae have a newcomer's organ located on the top rear of the abdomen that exudes a sugary solution (18%) that may also contain at least one amino acid. Flanking this organ are a pair of eversible tentacles that may attract the ants. While feeding on their host plant (whitethorn acacia), the larvae are attended by 13 species of ant. The ants obtain nutrients from the larvae and in return protect them from predators and parasitoids. After the larva goes through a final molt for the pupal stage, it crawls to the ground and searches for the nest of one the 13 ant species. It goes down into the nest and pupates. The ants touch and protect the pupa, but later, when the adult emerges, it only has two minutes to escape or it will be killed by the ants. The adult butterfly has no sugary fluid to appease the ants.

In Australia a related species, while emerging from the host ant nest, is protected by a cloak of long hairs that detach when grabbed by the ant. In the **Large Blue** of Europe, the last-stage larvae are carried into the underground nests by the ants, where the butterfly finishes its larval stage by eating ant larvae.

Eastern Tailed-Blue ♦ *Everes comyntas* 85a

KEY FIELD MARKS: *unh* with **a tail** and **two** submarginal orange spots.

SIZE: $5/8$–$1 1/8$ inches

ADULTS FLY: early March to November

HOST PLANTS: **lupine, clovers, vetch**

RANGE: south-central through southeastern Arizona (Also: CA, NV, UT, CO, NM)

HABITAT: open areas

SIMILAR SPECIES: **Western Tailed-Blue** *unh* has only **one** submarginal orange spot. Could superficially be confused as a hairstreak but lacks the *unh* blue spot of similar-looking species.

Western Tailed-Blue ♦ *Everes amyntula* 85b, c

KEY FIELD MARKS: *unh* with **a tail** and **one** submarginal spot (**85b**); *uph* (**85c**) with two orange submarginal spots

SIZE: $7/8$–$1 1/8$ inches

ADULTS FLY: late April to late August

HOST PLANTS: **purple loco, American vetch**

RANGE: northern and eastern Arizona (Also: CA, NV, UT, CO, NM)

HABITAT: open areas

SIMILAR SPECIES: **Eastern Tailed-Blue** *unh* has **two** submarginal orange spots. Could be superficially confused as a Hairstreak but lacks the *unh* blue spot of similar-looking species.

Dotted Blue ♦ *Euphilotes enoptes* 87a

KEY FIELD MARKS: *unh* red submarginal band capped outwardly with black spots.

SIZE: 1 inch

ADULTS FLY: September

HOST PLANT: **Wright's buckwheat**

RANGE: roughly northwestern Arizona (Also: CA, NV)

HABITAT: open areas near host plant

SIMILAR SPECIES: **Spalding's Blue** (page 88) and **Rita Blue** do not overlap in range. **Dotted Blue** lacks silvery submarginal spots of **Acmon Blue** (page 88).

Square-spotted Blue ♦ *Euphilotes battoides centralis* 87b

KEY FIELD MARKS: *uns* with an orange submarginal band capped outwardly with black spots; **spots squarish.**

SIZE: $^5/_8$–$^7/_8$ inch

ADULTS FLY: July to early August

HOST PLANT: **flat-top buckwheat**

RANGE: central to northwestern Arizona (Also: CA, NV)

HABITAT: open areas in mountains, open woodland

SIMILAR SPECIES: **Acmon Blue** (page 88) has silvery marginal black spots. **Rita Blue** *uns* spots are **not squarish.**

Rita Blue ♦ *Euphilotes rita* 87c

KEY FIELD MARKS: *unh* **orange submarginal band** capped outwardly with black spots.

SIZE: $^5/_8$–$^7/_8$ inch

ADULTS FLY: mid-August to late September (see note below)

HOST PLANTS: **Wright's buckwheat, wild buckwheat, sorrel buckwheat**

RANGE: north-central, central and eastern Arizona (Also: UT, CO, NM)

HABITAT: prairie, open areas, lower mountain canyons

SIMILAR SPECIES: **Square-spotted Blue** has *unh* **squarish** spots. **Acmon Blue** (page 88) *unh* has marginal **silvery black** spots.

NOTE: Subspecies *E. r. emmeli* in northeastern Arizona flies from late August to early September.

Spalding's Blue ♦ *Euphilotes spaldingi* 89a

KEY FIELD MARKS: *uns* orange submarginal band on **both** wings, capped outwardly with black spots.

SIZE: $3/4$–1 inch

ADULTS FLY: July

HOST PLANT: **red-root buckwheat**

RANGE: northern and northeastern to central-eastern Arizona (Also: NV, UT, CO, NM)

HABITAT: rocky areas near ponderosa pine and juniper woodlands

SIMILAR SPECIES: **Melissa Blue** *unh* has **iridescent** marginal spots. **Square-spotted Blue** *unf* (page 86) has **no** orange submarginal band.

Melissa Blue ♦ *Lycaeides melissa* 89b, c

KEY FIELD MARKS: *uns* (89b) with an orange submarginal band on **both** wings, capped outwardly with **silvery** black spots; female *ups* (89c) **brown** with an orange submarginal band on both wings.

SIZE: $7/8$–$1 1/4$ inches

ADULTS FLY: late April through early September

HOST PLANTS: **licorice, sweet vetch, Spanish clover, lupine** and **alfalfa**

RANGE: northwestern through central to central-eastern Arizona (Also: CA, NV, UT, CO, NM)

HABITAT: a wide variety of open habitats

SIMILAR SPECIES: **Spalding's Blue** lacks marginal *unh* **iridescent** spots.

Acmon Blue ♦ *Plebejus acmon* 89c

KEY FIELD MARKS: *unh* with **orange submarginal band** capped outwardly with **black silvery spots**; *uph* submarginal orange band.

SIZE: $3/4$–1 inch

ADULTS FLY: all year, weather permitting

HOST PLANTS: many species of **buckwheats** and **lotus**; **freckled milkvetch, sweet clover**

RANGE: throughout Arizona except the southwest (Also: CA, NV, UT, CO, NM)

HABITAT: desert, fields, mountain meadows

SIMILAR SPECIES: Both **Square-spotted Blue** (page 86) and **Rita Blue** (page 86) lack **silvery** black spots outwardly from the submarginal orange band. **Both Melissa Blue** and **Spalding's Blue** have orange spot bands on **both** *unf* and unh.

Silvery Blue ♦ *Glaucopsyche lygdamus* 91a

KEY FIELD MARKS: *unh* with **one row of black spots** surrounded by white; male *ups* silvery blue.

SIZE: $7/8$–$1\,1/8$ inches

ADULTS FLY: May through July

HOST PLANTS: **lupines, sweet vetch, vetch, purple loco, Spanish clover**

RANGE: throughout Arizona except southwest, south and extreme southeast (Also: CA, NV, UT, CO, NM)

HABITAT: mountain meadows and a variety of open areas

Small Blue ♦ *Philotiella speciosa* 91b

KEY FIELD MARKS: *unh* only three black spots (or few spots); *unf* **large rectangular black spot**.

SIZE: $5/8$–$3/4$ inch

ADULTS FLY: May to early June

HOST PLANTS: **kidney-leaved buckwheat**

RANGE: northwestern and extreme southwestern Arizona (Also: CA, NV, UT)

HABITAT: desert and dry washes

Arrowhead Blue ♦ *Glaucopsyche piasus* 91c

KEY FIELD MARKS: *unh* has eight or nine **white triangles** pointing towards the body,

SIZE: $7/8$–$1\,1/4$ inches

ADULTS FLY: late May to early July

HOST PLANT: **lupine**

RANGE: extreme north-central to northeastern Arizona (Also: CA, NV, UT, CO, NM)

HABITAT: meadows and sagebrush flats where the food plant grows

Arctic Blue ♦ *Agriades glandon* 93a, b, c

KEY FIELD MARKS: *unh* (93a) largest **white center spot is pentagonal and surrounded by tan** (better seen in California populations); male *upf* **blue** (93b) with wide black outside border and black dash; *uph* **blue with black submarginal spots at rear encased by black lines;** female *upf* (93c) **coppery-colored with dark veins** and narrow black border and black dash.

SIZE: $^7/_8$–1 inch

ADULTS FLY: July through August

HOST PLANTS: **rock jasmine, shooting star**

RANGE: close to the north-central border of Arizona across to the northeast and down close to the eastern border through the White Mountains (Also: CA, NV, UT, CO, NM)

HABITAT: mountain meadows, alpine areas

SIMILAR SPECIES: **Greenish Blue** (page 94) female *ups* **lacks dark veins;** male *uph* **lacks the more elaborate** spotting at rear.

Greenish Blue ♦ *Plebejus saepiolus* 95a, b, c

KEY FIELD MARKS: *unh* (95a, c) **some orange** in the double rows of submarginal spots; male (95b, c) *ups* blue with **wide black border** on outer *fw*; female *ups* copper-colored with orange submarginal band on each wing (not shown).

SIZE: 1–1 1/4 inches

ADULTS FLY: late May to early August

HOST PLANTS: several species of **clover**

RANGE: along the northern border of Arizona and down the eastern border through the White Mountains (Also: CA, NV, UT, CO, NM)

HABITAT: open areas, stream edges, mountain meadows

SIMILAR SPECIES: **Boisduval's Blue** (page 96) has no faint orange *unh* submarginal spots; in *upf* lacks the dash.

Boisduval's Blue ◆ *Plebejus icarioides* 97a, b, c, d

KEY FIELD MARKS: *unf* (**97a, b**) postmedian black spots *more prominent* than the tiny submarginal dots; *unh* black spots **surrounded by white** (**97a**) or only faint white spots (**97b**), usually a double row of submarginal spots but at the base there is **no orange** (as in **Greenish Blue**); lacks dash in *upf*; male *ups* (**97c**), female *ups* (**97d**).

SIZE: $7/8$–$1 1/4$ inches

ADULTS FLY: mid-June to mid-August

HOST PLANT: several species of **lupine**

RANGE: northern, central and eastern Arizona except the southeast (Also: CA, NV, UT, CO, NM)

HABITAT: mountain meadows, prairies and sagebrush flats—near **lupine**

SIMILAR SPECIES: **Greenish Blue** (page 94) usually has **orange** in the corner *unh* marginal spots; *upf* has dash.

Coppers ◆ Family Lycaeninae

The males are usually copper-colored above, hence the name, but in Arizona the names of the **Blue Copper** and **Purplish Copper** describe their upper wing color. Coppers usually bask with their wings open, have a flight that is not as erratic as the Hairstreaks, and usually hibernate as eggs. The males wait at flowers for their mates, rather than patrolling.

Ruddy Copper ◆ *Lycaena rubidus* 99

KEY FIELD MARKS: male *ups* (**99**) **bright orange-copper** with two dashes on *fw*; *unh* (**101a**) mostly gray with a few scattered black dots subtly encircled with white; female *ups* (**101b**) orange with brown or brown with black dots, orange band on the trailing edge of the *uph*.

SIZE: 1–1¼ inches

ADULTS FLY: June through August

HOST PLANTS: **western dock, wild rhubarb**

RANGE: only in the White Mountains on the central eastern border of Arizona (Also: CA, NV, UT, CO, NM)

HABITAT: meadows, gravelly dry washes

SIMILAR SPECIES: Female **Blue Copper** (page 102) has similar dot pattern but has no *uph* marginal orange band. Male **Purplish Copper** (page 100) *ups* has more black spots on copper-colored background.

NOTE: The **Ruddy Copper** in Arizona is a disjunct population that some authors consider a separate species.

Purplish Copper ◆ *Lycaena helloides* 101c, d

KEY FIELD MARKS: male *unh* has a dull **purplish cast** with a subtle submarginal orange band (**101c**); female *unh* similar but **lacks** purplish cast; male **ups** purplish with many black dots and solid **orange** marginal band; female **ups** dull **orange** with a wide brown *upf* margin (**101d**).

SIZE: $^7/_8$–1$^1/_4$ inches

ADULTS FLY: July through August

HOST PLANTS: several species of **knotweed, curly dock, wild rhubarb, sheep's sorrel**

RANGE: along the northern and northeastern to north-central border of Arizona (Also: CA, NV, UT, CO, NM)

HABITAT: meadows, stream edges

SIMILAR SPECIES: Male **Ruddy Copper** (page 98) is orange copper without black spots.

NOTE: This species is unusual for a Copper because it can have many broods.

Blue Copper ◆ *Lycaena heteronea* **103a, b, c**

KEY FIELD MARKS: male *ups* (**103a**) bright blue with **very narrow black border and black veins**; female *ups* (**103b**) gray with black spots; *unh* pearly with few or no black spots; *unf* (**103b**) has **more** black spots than Blues including two below median dash near the leading edge.

SIZE: 1–1$^1/_4$ inches

ADULTS FLY: mid-July through August

HOST PLANTS: **flat-top buckwheat, wild buckwheat**

RANGE: extreme north-central Arizona (Also CA, NV, UT, CO, NM)

HABITAT: open areas in mountains

SIMILAR SPECIES: Female **Ruddy Copper** (page 98) has *uph* orange marginal band. **Boisduval's Blue** (page 96) *unf* has no spots below median dash, black spots surrounded by white.

NOTE: This Copper acts and looks like a Blue, but anatomically it is closer to the Coppers.

Tailed Copper ◆ *Lycaena arota* **103d**

KEY FIELD MARKS: a Copper with a **tail**; male *ups* **all copper-colored**; female *ups* orange with a wide brown *fw* margin and scattered brown on both wings; *unh* a postmedian band composed of elongated spots edged with white; a submarginal white band.

SIZE: 1–1$^1/_4$ inches

ADULTS FLY: July through August

HOST PLANTS: **golden currant, trumpet gooseberry, wax currant**

RANGE: extreme northern Arizona (Also: CA, NV, UT, CO, NM)

HABITAT: woodland

NOTE: the only Copper in Arizona with a tail

Metalmarks ◆ Family Riodinidae

The shiny metallic markings in some species have given this family its common name. In adult males the front leg is less than half the length of the other legs (see **107c** *uns* of **Palmer's Metalmark**). Females have three pairs of legs of equal length. The Metalmarks superficially resemble Checkerspots but have a more angular shape and usually have long antennae, sometimes held together in front. The Metalmarks also have associations with ants, as in the Lycaeninae, but the positions of the honey glands and other structures differ. Hibernation is as a larva or pupa. The Metalmarks are a predominantly tropical group with over 1000 species. Of the 19 species in North America, 10 have been found in Arizona.

Mormon Metalmark ◆ *Apodemia mormo* 105, 107a

KEY FIELD MARKS: *ups* (**105**) orange ground absent on outer edge of wings, **two** rows of **submarginal white dots**; *uns* (**107a**) **large white irregular patches bordered by black**. In the race *mejicana* there is much more orange on the *unh* than in nominate *mormo*. See note below.

SIZE: 1–1¼ inches

ADULTS FLY: late February to mid-November

HOST PLANTS: many species of *Eriogonum*

RANGE: throughout Arizona except the extreme southwest (Also: CA, NV, UT, CO, NM).

HABITAT: a variety of open areas

SIMILAR SPECIES: **Palmer's** (page 106) and **Nais Metalmarks** (page 108) *ups* have a marginal orange band.

NOTE: Two species may be involved in Arizona, with the two different forms flying in overlapping locations at different times.

Palmer's Metalmark ◆ *Apodemia palmeri* **10b, c**

KEY FIELD MARKS: *ups* (**107b**) **orange** ground **along edge** of both wings, **one** row of white spots on the outer edge; *upf* postmedian white band curves outward; *uns* (**107c**) white patches bordered by pale orange-brown.

SIZE: $5/8$–$7/8$ inch

ADULT'S FLY: late April to mid-November

HOST PLANTS: **mesquites**

RANGE: west of a diagonal line from the northwest corner to central eastern Arizona (Also: CA, UT, NM).

HABITAT: thorn-scrub, desert, washes

SIMILAR SPECIES: **Mormon Metalmark** (page 104) *ups* dark band. **Nais Metalmark** (page 108) *ups* lacks white spots on outer edge.

Nais Metalmark ◆ *Apodemia nais* 109a, b

KEY FIELD MARKS: *ups* (**109a**) **black** circles in **orange marginal** band; *upf* white postmedian band straight, bordered by black; *unh* (**109b**) two orange bands bordered by intermittent black spots.

SIZE: $1-1^1/_4$ inches

ADULTS FLY: mid-June to mid-August

HOST PLANT: **buck brush**

RANGE: north-central to east central to southeastern Arizona (Also: CO, NM).

HABITAT: open mountain slopes

SIMILAR SPECIES: **Mormon Metalmark** *ups* (page 104) has black edge. **Palmer's Metalmark** *ups* (page 106) has submarginal white spots.

Hepburn's Metalmark ◆ *Apodemia hepburni* 109c

KEY FIELD MARKS: *ups* ground **predominantly gray, faint black spots** in marginal orange; *uns* similar to **Palmer's Metalmark.**

SIZE: $^7/_8$ inch

ADULTS FLY: a rare influx species; one certain August record

HOST PLANTS: not known in Arizona

RANGE: to be looked for in extreme southeastern Arizona

HABITAT: desert washes

SIMILAR SPECIES: **Palmer's Metalmark** (page 106) has *ups* **white submarginal dots** that are missing in **Hepburn's.**

NOTE: Smaller butterfly is a **Ceraunus Blue.**

Fatal Metalmark ◆ *Calephelis nemesis* **111a, b**

KEY FIELD MARKS: *ups* (**111a**) **dark** medial band; *uph* **absence** of dark subterminal dots; **uns** (**111b**) very similar to **Arizona Metalmark**.

SIZE: $3/4$–1 inch

ADULTS FLY: all year, weather permitting

HOST PLANT: **seep willow**

RANGE: along the western border and across central and southern Arizona to the southeast (Also: CA, UT, NM)

HABITAT: desert creeks, canyons, chaparral

SIMILAR SPECIES: **Arizona** and **Wright's Metalmarks** (page 112) lack the dark postmedian band and have **more prominent** silvery bands.

Arizona Metalmark ◆ *Calephelis arizonensis* **111c, d**

KEY FIELD MARKS: *ups* (**111c**) silvery postmedian and submarginal bands; *uns* (**111d**) very similar to **Wright's** and **Fatal Metalmarks**.

SIZE: $3/4$–1 inch

ADULTS FLY: all year, weather permitting

HOST PLANT: *Bidens* species

RANGE: southeastern Arizona

HABITAT: desert foothills

SIMILAR SPECIES: **Fatal Metalmark:** duller with dark median band. **Wright's Metalmark** (page112) has sinuous *fw* edge (no overlap in range).

Ares Metalmark ◆ *Emesis ares* 113a

KEY FIELD MARKS: *upf* uniform color with black dots on outer edge; *uns* very similar to **Zela Metalmark**.

SIZE: $1^1/_8$–$1^1/_4$ inches

ADULTS FLY: mid-July to late September

HOST PLANT: **Mexican blue oak**

RANGE: southeastern Arizona (Also NM)

HABITAT: streams and canyons in mountain foothills

SIMILAR SPECIES: **Zela Metalmark** (page 114) has dark median rectangle on *upf* and lacks submarginal spots on *upf.*

Wright's Metalmark ◆ *Calephelis wrighti* 113b, c

KEY FIELD MARKS: *fw* sinuous edge; *ups* (**113b**) silvery postmedian and submarginal bands; *uns* (**113c**) very similar to **Arizona** and **Fatal Metalmarks**.

SIZE: 1–$1^1/_8$ inches

ADULTS FLY: February to December

HOST PLANT: **sweetbush**

RANGE: along the western border of Arizona (Also: CA, NV)

HABITAT: desert washes

SIMILAR SPECIES: **Fatal Metalmark** (page 110): duller and with dark median band. **Arizona Metalmark** (page 110) does not overlap in range.

Zela Metalmark ◆ *Emesis zela* 115a, b

KEY FIELD MARKS: *upf* (**115a**) large gray rectangle at mid-costa, no dots on outer edge; *uns* (**115b**) very similar to **Ares Metalmark**.

SIZE: 1–1^1/$_4$ inches

ADULTS FLY: February to mid-September

HOST PLANT: not known, but **oak** is suspected

RANGE: through the central portion of Arizona to the central east and southeast (Also: NM)

HABITAT: streams and canyons in mountain foothills

SIMILAR SPECIES: **Ares Metalmark** (page 112) has uniformly colored *upf* with dark submarginal spots.

Brush-footed Butterflies ◆ Family Nymphalidae

This is a very large family and is broken up into subfamilies, of which those occurring in Arizona are listed above. A major characteristic of the family is the reduced pair of front legs, the so called "brush-feet." It is rare to readily see this brush-foot in the field. One very windy day, the senior author followed a buffeted **American Lady (117)** into deep grass. Taking advantage of a natural moment, where one of the Lady's brush-feet had inadvertently been held outward by a grass stem, he took this photograph. Although both males and females of Nymphalidae have these shortened front legs, the females use the sharp tip of the foot to test the chemistry of their host plants. One can observe this quick repeated flashing out of the brush-feet onto the leaf surface.

Snouts ◆ Subfamily Libytheinae

American Snout ◆ *Libytheana carinenta* 119a, b

KEY FIELD MARKS: palps very long; *ups:* narrow *upf* with **squared off apex** and scalloped margin; *upf* two large orange basal patches; *uph* one large orange patch; *unf* showing **basal orange** and white patches if it is held up, but with *fw* closed the mottled unh gives perfect camouflage.

SIZE: $1^3/_8$–$1^7/_8$ inches

ADULTS FLY: all year, weather permitting

HOST PLANTS: **desert** and **netleaf hackberries**

RANGE: throughout Arizona (Also: CA, NV, UT, CO, NM)

HABITAT: desert and upland arroyos and urban areas

NOTE: The elongated palps (which enclose the proboscis) are characteristic of the subfamily Libytheinae. They serve to accentuate the camouflage when the wings are closed, as seen in the mating pair on a grass stem.

Heliconians and Fritillaries ◆ Subfamily Heliconiinae

Gulf Fritillary ◆ *Agraulis vanillae* 121a, b

KEY FIELD MARKS: *ups* (**121a**) **bright orange**, *upf* usually with **three white spots** surrounded with black along leading edge; *unf* (**121b**) with **large silvery spots**.

SIZE: $2^3/_4$–$3^1/_4$ inches

ADULTS FLY: April through October

HOST PLANTS: several species of **passion flower**

RANGE: throughout except the northeast quarter of Arizona (Also: CA, NV, UT, CO, NM)

HABITAT: wide variety of habitats including urban areas

Zebra Heliconian ◆ *Heliconius charithonia* 123

KEY FIELD MARKS: *ups* **four yellow stripes** on black.

SIZE: $2^1/_2$–$3^5/_8$ inches

ADULTS FLY: uncommon influx species late April to late May and early August to mid-November

HOST PLANTS: **passion flower** suspected in Arizona

RANGE: southeastern Arizona (Also: CO, NM)

HABITAT: river edges

Variegated Fritillary ◆ *Euptoieta claudia* 125a, b

KEY FIELD MARKS: *ups* **125a** an orange and black checkered pattern with a submarginal row of **black dots** and a **marginal black band**; *unh* **125b** with a **wide obvious creamy** postmedial band.

SIZE: $1^3/_8$–$2^3/_4$ inches

ADULTS FLY: all year, weather permitting

HOST PLANTS: **passion flower**, **spiderling**, *Hybanthus*, *Metastelma*

RANGE: throughout Arizona (Also: CA, NV, UT, CO, NM)

HABITAT: a wide variety of open areas, washes, fields, prairies, gardens

SIMILAR SPECIES: **Mexican Fritillary** (page 126): base of *uph* is plain orange with **no** black lines; *unh* postmedial band **faint and indistinct**.

Mexican Fritillary *Euptoieta hegesia* 127a, b

KEY FIELD MARKS: *ups* (**127a**) similar to **Variegated Fritillary**, except basal portion of **Mexican Fritillary lacks a pattern**; *unh* (**127b**) similar to **Variegated Fritillary**, except postmedial band in **Mexican Fritillary** is **very faint**.

SIZE: $2^1/_2$–3 inches

ADULTS FLY: mid-June to late November

HOST PLANT: **passion flower**

RANGE: southeastern Arizona (Also: CA, NV, UT, CO, NM)

HABITAT: a wide variety of open areas, gardens

Nokomis Fritillary ◆ *Speyeria nokomis* 129a, b, 131a

KEY FIELD MARKS: *unh* (131a) ground color of basal two-thirds is **brown** with all spots **silvery**, submarginal spots are flattened ovals with small brown triangles above and **wide yellow** postmedial band; female *ups* black and white pattern (129b); male (129a) .

SIZE: 2^1/$_2$–3 inches

ADULTS FLY: August through October

HOST PLANT: **meadow violet**

RANGE: originally found in local colonies in the eastern quarter of Arizona; now probably extirpated south of the White Mountains (Also: CA, NV, UT, CO, NM)

HABITAT: meadows and marshes in mountains

NOTES: The Fritillaries in the genus *Speyeria* are notoriously difficult to tell apart and are very variable within each species. Females must find violets, often when the plant has died back but is still alive underground. Somehow the female knows where the host plant is. It appears, however, that she lays her eggs haphazardly on the ground in the fall. The eggs hatch and hibernate as unfed larvae through-out the winter. In the spring they find the emerging violet, eat the leaves and then pupate. In Arizona the Fritillary adults fly through October, delaying their egg laying to benefit the survival of their offspring.

Mormon Fritillary ◆ *Speyeria mormonia* 131b

KEY FIELD MARKS: *unh* ground color is pale yellow throughout with all spots **cream-colored** (not silvery).

SIZE: 1⁵/₈–2 inches

ADULTS FLY: July and August

HOST PLANT: **violets**

RANGE: White Mountains of eastern Arizona (Also: CA, NV, UT, CO, NM)

HABITAT: mountain meadows

SIMILAR SPECIES: All other **Fritillaries** in Arizona have **silvery *unh*** spots.

Coronis Fritillary ◆ *Speyeria coronis* 133a, b

KEY FIELD MARKS: *unh* postmedian band straw-colored or pale buff.

SIZE: 2–2$^1/_2$ inches

ADULTS FLY: late June through September

HOST PLANT: **Nuttall's violet**

RANGE: extreme north-central Arizona (Also: CA, NV, UT, CO)

HABITAT: brushy open areas

Atlantis Fritillary ◆ *Speyeria atlantis* 135a, b

KEY FIELD MARKS: *unh* basal two-thirds brown/reddish-brown, spots silvery with submarginal spots large rounded triangles, yellow submarginal band narrow (**135b**).

SIZE: 2–2³/₄ inches

ADULTS FLY: early July to mid-August

HOST PLANTS: **violets**

RANGE: roughly east of a line running from the northwest (except for the extreme northwest) to the southeast of Arizona as far south as the Pinaleños (Also: CA, NV, UT, CO, NM)

HABITAT: mountain meadows

SIMILAR SPECIES: **Aphrodite Fritillary** *uns* not separable

Aphrodite Fritillary ◆ *Speyeria aphrodite* 135c

KEY FIELD MARKS: *unh* very similar to **Atlantis Fritillary**

SIZE: 2¹/₄–3 inches

ADULTS FLY: July and August

HOST PLANTS: **violets**

RANGE: White Mountains in eastern Arizona (Also: UT, CO, NM)

HABITAT: mountain meadows

SIMILAR SPECIES: *unh* of **Atlantis Fritillary** not separable; *ups* of Atlantis has darker wing base and males have thicker black around the veins; females have more white on *fw* edge. Much more local than the widespread **Atlantis Fritillary** which starts flying a month earlier.

True Brush-foots ♦ Subfamily Nymphalinae

Arachne Checkerspot ♦ *Polydryas arachne* 137a, b

KEY FIELD MARKS: *ups* (**137a**) an orange and black pattern with a black marginal band and a banded dark orange–light orange alternating pattern. **Note: two black dots** in *hw* submarginal band (second band from the rear); *unf* **three rows** of creamy spots near apex, the inner row smaller; *unh* (**137b**) **creamy** marginal band.

SIZE: $1^1/_8$–$1^1/_2$ inches

ADULTS FLY: mid-April to late October

HOST PLANTS: several species of **penstemon**

RANGE: throughout except central west to southwest portion of state (Also: CA, NV, UT, CO, NM)

HABITAT: oak woodland, mesquite forest, pine woodland

SIMILAR SPECIES: **Sagebrush Checkerspot** (page 138) **lacks** black dots on lower *uph*, has only **two rows** of creamy spots *unf* apex, has orange *unh* marginal band. **Variable Checkerspot** (page 140) has white spots on abdomen.

Sagebrush Checkerspot ♦ *Chlosyne acastus* 139a, b

KEY FIELD MARKS: *ups* (**139a**) an orange and black checkerspot pattern; *uph* margin is **orange** with a **narrow black line** on either side; *unf* (**139b**) **two rows of creamy spots** at apex with **orange** marginal band.

SIZE: 1$\frac{1}{4}$–1$\frac{1}{2}$ inches

ADULTS FLY: mid-February to late May; late brood in September

HOST PLANTS: **hoary aster, yellow rabbitbrush**

RANGE: throughout Arizona except extreme southwest to extreme south-central (Also: CA, NV, UT, CO, NM)

HABITAT: streambeds, oak woodland, sagebrush

SIMILAR SPECIES: See **Arachne Checkerspot** (page 136).

Variable Checkerspot ♦ *Euphydryas chalcedona* 141a, b

Includes *anicia* and *klotzi* (**143a**); see note below. *E. c. anicia* high mountain form **141a**; *E. c. anicia* desert form **141b**.

KEY FIELD MARKS: *ups* a black and white Checkerspot with some **red** spots; **white spots** on abdomen; *unf* two rows of creamy spots near apex.

SIZE: $1^{1}/_{8}$–$2^{1}/_{8}$ inches

ADULTS FLY: mid-February to mid-May, October

HOST PLANTS: a wide variety of plants in the **figwort** family including **Indian paintbrushes, penstemons, monkeyflower, bee plant, lousewort, hedge-nettle** and **mullein**

RANGE: most of Arizona except extreme southwest to extreme south-central (Also: CA, NV, UT, CO, NM)

HABITAT: a wide variety of open habitats

SIMILAR SPECIES: *uns* of **Sagebrush Checkerspot** (page 138) very similar but note *unf* second row of sub-apex creamy spots is limited to two. *unh* margin of **Arachne Checkerspot** (page 136) is **cream-colored**. *ups* of both of these Checkerspots very similar, while **Variable Checkerspot** usually has more distinctive **red-orange** patches and has **white spots** on the abdomen.

NOTE: There are at least two forms in Arizona, *anicia* and *klotzi*, that may be two different species.

Variable Checkerspot ♦ *Euphydryas chalcedona*

E. c. klotzi **ups** (**143a**)

E. c. chalcedona **uns** (**143b**)

Theona Checkerspot ♦ *Thessalia theona* 145a, b

KEY FIELD MARKS: *uph* (**145a**) **banded** from margin with black, orange and yellow; *unh* (**145b**) neatly banded orange and cream-colored.

SIZE: 1–1^1/$_2$ inches

ADULTS FLY: mid-March to late October

HOST PLANTS: **Indian paintbrush**, *Brachystigma*

RANGE: across central Arizona to and including the south-central, central-east and southeast (Also: NM)

HABITAT: scrub, mountain foothills

SIMILAR SPECIES: Similar to **Crescents** and other **Checkerspots** but the **orderly** bands on the *ups* and *uns* are distinctive.

Black Checkerspot ♦ *Thessalia cyneas* 147a, b

KEY FIELD MARKS: *ups* (**147a**) **black** ground color with **two yellow bands** and a submarginal orange band; *unh* (**147b**) yellowish with **a black postmedian band** with **yellowish** circles inside, **continuing on** *unf.*

SIZE: 1–1$\frac{1}{2}$ inches

ADULTS FLY: March to early November

HOST PLANT: Indian paintbrush

RANGE: southeastern Arizona—in the Huachuca Mountains, but there are also a few records from the Mule, Dragoon and Chiricahua Mountains (Also: NM)

HABITAT: foothills, canyons, ridges

Fulvia Checkerspot ♦ *Thessalia fulvia* 149a, b

KEY FIELD MARKS: *ups* (**149a**) a white to yellow postmedian and submarginal band on orange ground color; *unh* (**149b**) cream-colored with a black postmedian band with creamy circles inside; *unf* the inside cream-colored spot band has **no black border** on the **inside** edge.

SIZE: 1–1³/₈ inches

ADULTS FLY: March to late June; August

HOST PLANT: **Indian paintbrush**

RANGE: most of Arizona except extreme northwest, southwest and south-central (Also: UT, CO, NM)

HABITAT: foothills, ridges, prairie

SIMILAR SPECIES: **Black Checkerspot** (page 146) has *ups* **black** ground color and *unf* submarginal band has **black inner border**.

Leanira Checkerspot ♦ *Thessalia leanira* 151a

KEY FIELD MARKS: *ups* orange with submarginal **yellowish** spot band; *uns* very similar to **Fulvia Checkerspot**; palpi **orange**

SIZE: 1$\frac{1}{4}$–1$\frac{5}{8}$ inches

ADULTS FLY: April through June

HOST PLANT: **Indian paintbrush**

RANGE: extreme northwestern Arizona (Also: CA, NV, UT)

HABITAT: oak-juniper woodland

SIMILAR SPECIES: *ups* and *uns* **Fulvia Checkerspot** (page 148) very similar but palpi are **black and white**.

California Patch ♦ *Chlosyne californica* 151b, c

KEY FIELD MARKS: *ups* (**151a**) with a **broad** orange median band and an **orange spotted** submarginal band; *unf* **orange** postmedian patch; *unh* (**151c**) three vertical yellowish bands, the middle one widest

SIZE: 1$\frac{1}{4}$–1$\frac{3}{4}$

ADULTS FLY: March through November

HOST PLANTS: **golden-eye, common sunflower**

RANGE: western one-quarter of Arizona except for the extreme southwest corner (Also: CA, NV, UT)

HABITAT: desert washes and scrub

SIMILAR SPECIES: **Bordered Patch** (page 152) **lacks** *ups* orange submarginal band; *unh* median band **narrower** and **lacks** *upf* orange patch.

Bordered Patch ♦ *Chlosyne lacinia* 153a, b, c

KEY FIELD MARKS: *ups* (**153b**) dark brown to black with a **variably white** (**153c**) **to orange** median band that is **also variable in width** (in some individuals reduced to a line of spots or, rarely, entirely absent); *unh* three vertical yellowish bands with orange patch in corner (**153a**).

SIZE: $1^1/_4$–$1^7/_8$ inches

ADULTS FLY: late January to mid-November

HOST PLANTS: **ragweed, blanket flower, sunflowers, golden-eye, crown beard**

RANGE: western, central and southern Arizona (Also: CA, NV, UT, NM)

HABITAT: desert washes, mesquite woodland

SIMILAR SPECIES: See **California Patch** (page 150).

NOTE: This species can be amazingly variable, especially the *ups*.

Silvery Checkerspot ◆ *Chlosyne nycteis* 155a, b

KEY FIELD MARKS: *ups* (**155a**) with a broad white median band; *uph* black submarginal spots with silver centers; *unh* (**155b**) dark spots with white centers in the dark area of the outer margin.

SIZE: 1$^{1}/_{8}$–1$^{3}/_{4}$ inches

ADULTS FLY: June to mid-July

HOST PLANT: **coneflower**

RANGE: roughly around and along the Mogollon Rim in central Arizona through the White Mountains in the east (Also: CO, NM)

HABITAT: clearings near streams, scrub and woodland

SIMILAR SPECIES: **Theona Checkerspot** (page 144) **lacks** *uph* submarginal black spots with silver centers and has *ups* yellow median band. Other **Crescents** by *unh* **lacking** white-centered submarginal spots.

Tiny Checkerspot ♦ *Dymasia dymas* 157a, b

KEY FIELD MARKS: *upf* (**157a**) with a prominent **white rectangle** on leading edge; *unh* (**157b**) seven large white submarginal spots with a **narrow black** marginal band.

SIZE: $^7/_8$–$1^1/_8$ inches

ADULTS FLY: all year, weather permitting

HOST PLANTS: *Tetramerium, Justicia*

RANGE: west-central and southern Arizona (Also: CA, NM)

HABITAT: desert, scrub, washes and streams

SIMILAR SPECIES: **Elada Checkerspot** *upf* lacks white spot on leading edge; *unh* has orange marginal band.

Elada Checkerspot ♦ *Texola elada* 157c, d

KEY FIELD MARKS: *ups* (**157c**) very similar to **Tiny Checkerspot** but **lacks** white rectangle on leading edge *upf*; *unh* (**157d**) similar to **Tiny Checkerspot** but with an **orange** marginal band.

SIZE: $^7/_8$–$1^1/_8$ inches

ADULTS FLY: mid-March to early December

HOST PLANT: **desert honeysuckle**

RANGE: west-central and southern Arizona (Also: CA, NM)

HABITAT: desert, scrub, mesquite woodland, washes

SIMILAR SPECIES: See **Tiny Checkerspot** with which it sometimes flies.

Texan Crescent ♦ *Phyciodes texana* 159a, b

KEY FIELD MARKS: *fw* (**159a**) outer edge is **indented**; *uph* two rows of white spots; *unf* (**159b**) orange basal portion; *unh* white postmedian band.

SIZE: 1^1/$_4$–1^1/$_2$ inches

ADULTS FLY: all year, weather permitting

HOST PLANT: *Dicliptera*

RANGE: roughly the southern quarter of Arizona and up the extreme western border (Also: CA, NV, NM, CO)

HABITAT: streams, dry washes, gardens

SIMILAR SPECIES: Differs from all the other **Crescents** in having indented *fw*, black and white *ups*, and *unf* orange at the base with wide black postmedian band.

Tawny Crescent ♦ *Phyciodes batesii* 159c

KEY FIELD MARKS: Very similar to the **Pearl Crescent**, which has a more southerly range in Arizona with no overlap.

SIZE: 1–1^1/$_2$ inches

ADULTS FLY: May to early July

HOST PLANTS: species of *Aster*

RANGE: north-central (Kaibab Plateau) and the extreme northeastern corner of Arizona (Four Corners) (Also: UT, CO, NM)

HABITAT: rocky ridges, ravines

Vesta Crescent ◆ *Phyciodes vesta* 161a, b, c

KEY FIELD MARKS: *unf* (**161a, c**) lower submarginal band **chain-like**—orange edged with black, many narrow black parallel lines

SIZE: $1^1/_4$–$1^1/_2$ inches

ADULTS FLY: late March to early May and early August to early November (two broods)

HOST PLANT: *Dyschoriste*

RANGE: southeastern Arizona (Also: NM, CO)

HABITAT: streams, mesquite woodland

SIMILAR SPECIES: No other **Crescent** has chain-like pattern on *unf*.

Phaon Crescent ♦ *Phyciodes phaon* 163a, b, c

KEY FIELD MARKS: male *upf* (**163a**) **three bands**—black, yellow and orange—just outside the four orange rectangles; *unh* (**163b, c**) females cream-colored, *unh* male tan, both with **several dark smudges** including the outer margin.

SIZE: 1–1$\frac{1}{4}$ inches

ADULTS FLY: mid-May to mid-October

HOST PLANTS: **frog fruit**

RANGE: central-western and southwestern to southeastern Arizona (also: CA, NM, CO)

HABITAT: a wide variety of open areas

Pearl Crescent ♦ *Phyciodes tharos* 165a, b

KEY FIELD MARKS: male *uph* (**165a**) mostly **orange at base**; *upf* orange post-median rectangles taper to the costa; male *unh* (**165b**) tan with no smudges other than the outer edge.

SIZE: 1–1$^3/_8$ inches

ADULTS FLY: late March to mid-November

HOST PLANTS: **Asters**

RANGE: from central Arizona to the southeast; a disjunct population along the lower Colorado River (Also: CA, NM, CO, UT, NV)

HABITAT: a wide variety of open areas, streams

SIMILAR SPECIES: See **Northern Crescent** (page 166). **Phaon** (page 162), **Northern** and **Vesta Crescents** (page 160) *unh* have leading edge smudge.

Painted Crescent ♦ *Phyciodes picta* 165c, 167c

KEY FIELD MARKS: *upf* (**165c**) four roundish spots at sub-apex that taper in size to the costa, four or five white postmedian rectangular spots that also taper slightly to the costa; *unh* (**167c**) **cream-colored** with **lack of contrasting lines, spots or smudges**.

SIZE: $^7/_8$–1$^1/_4$ inches

ADULTS FLY: late February to late October

HOST PLANTS: **field bindweed** and possibly *Symphyotrichum subulatum*, a Daisy

RANGE: central and eastern Arizona (also: UT, CO, NM)

HABITAT: open and marshy areas, streams, gardens, roadsides

Northern Crescent ◆ *Phyciodes selenis* 167a, b

KEY FIELD MARKS: *ups* (**167a**) mostly orange with a ***wide black border***, orange patches not divided by black bands or lines; *unh* (**167b**) **yellowish** with an **orange smudge** at the outer margin and another smaller orange smudge along the upper edge; *unf* orange ground color.

SIZE: $1^1/_4$–$1^5/_8$ inches

ADULTS FLY: June and July

HOST PLANTS: **Asters**

RANGE: north-central and northeastern Arizona, south and east to the White Mountains (Also: NM, NV, UT, CO)

SIMILAR SPECIES: **Pearl Crescent** (page 164): little or no overlap in Arizona; *ups* orange patches **divided** by black bands or lines; *unh* **lacks** costal smudge; *unf* **tan-colored** ground. All other similar Crescents have **less orange** in *ups*.

Field Crescent ♦ *Phyciodes campestris* 169a, b

KEY FIELD MARKS: *ups* (**169a**) **dark base to** *hw*; *fw* **with black areas**; *unh* (**169b**) all pale (no dark smudges); *unf* **narrow yellow bar** in orange in lower part.

SIZE: 1–1^1/$_2$ inches

ADULTS FLY: late February to late September

HOST PLANTS: **asters**

RANGE: north of the Mogollon Rim and in the White Mountains of Arizona (Also: CA, NM, CO, UT, NV)

HABITAT: open areas in mountains and foothills, streams

SIMILAR SPECIES: **Mylitta** (page 170) and **Pale Crescent** (page 168) **lack** black base to *uph*.

Pale Crescent ♦ *Phyciodes pallida* 169c, d

KEY FIELD MARKS: *upf* similar to **Mylitta Crescent** but **Pale Crescent** has a **large black median spot near the** *hw*; females *ups* has yellow-orange postmedian band.

SIZE: 1^1/$_8$–1^1/$_2$ inches

ADULTS FLY: late June through early August

HOST PLANTS: **thistles**

RANGE: north-central Arizona (Also: NV, UT, CO)

SIMILAR SPECIES: **Mylitta Crescent** (page 170) **lacks** large black *upf* median spot near *hw*.

Mylitta Crescent ◆ *Phyciodes mylitta* 171a, b, c, d

KEY FIELD MARKS: *ups* variable; females (**171a, b, c**) have yellow-orange post-median band; *uph* upper dark line above black submarginal spots is often broken; *unh* often a white postmedian band (**171d**); *unf* lacking dark spots (except one in mid-rear).

SIZE: 1–1^1/$_2$ inches

ADULTS FLY: late February to late September

HOST PLANTS: **thistles, seep spring monkeyflower**

RANGE: throughout Arizona except west-central through southwestern (Also: CA, NM, CO, UT, NV)

HABITAT: streams meadows or other open areas of foothills and mountains

SIMILAR SPECIES: **Field Crescent** (page 168) has black at base *hw*, *unf* with a **narrow yellow bar** at leading edge and three or four black spots near bottom. **Pale Crescent** (page 168) has large *upf* black median spot near *hw*.

Question Mark ♦ *Polygonia interrogationis* 173a

KEY FIELD MARKS: *ups* violet edge *fw* and *hw*; *uph* extensive **black** on inner half (wet-season form); *upf*—look for the mid-costal large spot: under it and to the outside is a **black slanted compressed oval** with a round spot under it (other Commas lack this oval spot).

SIZE: 1^7/$_8$–2^1/$_2$ inches

ADULTS FLY: early August to early November

HOST PLANT: **netleaf hackberry**

RANGE: southeastern Arizona (also: NM, CO)

HABITAT: watercourses with food plant, towns

NOTE: Dry-season form *hw* is orangish brown not black.

Satyr Comma ♦ *Polygonia satyrus* 173b, c

KEY FIELD MARKS: *upf* (**173b**) the **third inner spot** down from the costa has a **satellite smudge** above and to the outside (other Commas do not have this smudge); *uph* has four black spots, outer edge light-colored; *unh* (**173c**) brownish with silver comma.

SIZE: 1^3/$_4$–2 inches

ADULTS FLY: late February to mid-November

HOST PLANTS: **nettle, willow**

RANGE: throughout Arizona except the southwest desert (Also: CA, NV, UT, CO, NM)

HABITAT: rivers, streams, and nearby open areas

NOTE: All the **Commas** (named for the white "comma" in the central *hw*), also called **Anglewings**, have irregular edges to the wings which when closed look like tattered leaves.

Green Comma ♦ *Polygonia faunus* 175a, b

KEY FIELD MARKS: *ups* (**175a**) a wide **dark edge**, conspicuous **yellow** sub-marginal marks on the *hw*; *uns* (**175b**) conspicuous postmedian and sub-marginal **green** spots, dark areas scattered.

SIZE: 1³/₈–2 inches

ADULTS FLY: late June to mid-August

HOST PLANT: **quaking aspen**

RANGE: two isolated populations in Arizona, one in the mountains south of Flagstaff and the other in the White Mountains (Also: CA, UT, NM)

HABITAT: openings and streams in coniferous forests

SIMILAR SPECIES: **Hoary** (page 176) and **Satyr Comma** (page 172): *uph* has **light margin**; *uns* of *Hoary* has dark base uniform **gray** outer half; *uns* of **Satyr brown**.

Hoary Comma ♦ *Polygonia gracilis* 177a, b

KEY FIELD MARKS: *uph* (**177a**) two black spots on inner base, light edge to outer margin; *uns* (**177b**) darker base contrasts with gray outer margin.

SIZE: 1$\frac{1}{2}$–1$\frac{7}{8}$ inches

ADULTS FLY: May through September

HOST PLANTS: **currant, gooseberry**

RANGE: mountains of central, eastern and northern Arizona (Also: CA, NV, UT, CO, NM)

HABITAT: streams and nearby open areas in coniferous woodland

SIMILAR SPECIES: See **Green Comma** (page 174).

California Tortoiseshell ♦ *Nymphalis californica* 179a, b

KEY FIELD MARKS: *upf* (**179a**) outer black costal spot has **white** on either side; *uns* (**179b**) dark brown base contrasting with lighter brown outer half, a dark subterminal band.

SIZE: 1³/₄–2¹/₈ inches

ADULTS FLY: early March to early August

HOST PLANTS: **deerbrush, buckbrush**

RANGE: throughout except for the southwestern third of Arizona (Also: CA, NV, UT, CO, NM)

HABITAT: mountains, open areas, brushland

SIMILAR SPECIES: *unh* of **Commas** have silver "comma."

Milbert's Tortoiseshell ♦ *Nymphalis milberti* 179c, d

KEY FIELD MARKS: *ups* (**179c**) dark base, broad yellow-orange postmedian band, bright blue *hw* submarginal spots; *uns* (**179d**) black with brown postmedian band.

SIZE: 1¹/₂–2 inches

ADULTS FLY: early July to late August in southeast Arizona, May to October in the White Mountains

HOST PLANT: **nettle**

RANGE: northern and northeastern Arizona south to the Pinaleño Mountains (Also: CA, NV, UT, CO, NM)

HABITAT: meadows, streams in mountains

American Lady ♦ *Vanessa virginiensis* 181a, b

KEY FIELD MARKS: *upf* (181a) usually a white rectangle (in this individual it is orange) along costa edge inside the white subapex spots, a **white** dot (sometimes absent) in the largest outer orange rectangle, dark lines on the inner wing unconnected; *uph* submarginal spots fused (sometimes all of them); *unh* (181b) two large submarginal spots.

SIZE: 1³/₄–2¹/₄ inches

ADULTS FLY: all year, weather permitting

HOST PLANTS: **cud weeds, thistles, Nettle**

RANGE: throughout Arizona except the southwest (Also: CA, NV, UT, CO, NM)

HABITAT: a wide variety of open areas

SIMILAR SPECIES: **Painted Lady** (page 182): dark pattern on inner *upf* **connected,** *uph* black submarginal dots **not fused together. West Coast Lady** (page 184): all *uph* submarginal spots with **blue centers.**

Painted Lady ◆ *Vanessa cardui* 183a, b

KEY FIELD MARKS: *ups* (**183a**) **white** rectangle in outer costa, inner brown band **connected**; *uph* four round **black** submarginal spots; *unh* (**183b**) **four** submarginal iridescent spots; *unf* two white rectangles along the costal edge.

SIZE: $1^3/_4$–$2^1/_2$ inches

ADULTS FLY: all year, weather permitting

HOST PLANTS: many species in the sunflower family

RANGE: throughout Arizona (also CA, NV, UT, CO, NM)

HABITAT: a wide variety of open areas from deserts to high mountains, gardens

SIMILAR SPECIES: See **American Lady** (page 180).

NOTES: **Painted Ladies** can make migration-like movements, sometimes in immense numbers. This species can be found on all continents except Australia and Antarctica.

West Coast Lady ♦ *Vanessa annabella* 185a, b

KEY FIELD MARKS: *upf* (**185a**) outermost costal rectangle **orange**; *uph* four submarginal round spots with **blue centers**; *unf* yellowish costal rectangle, red-orange base; *unh* (**185b**) **four** iridescent submarginal circles.

SIZE: $1^1/_2$–$1^7/_8$ inches

ADULTS FLY: all year, weather permitting

HOST PLANTS: **cheeseweed, mallows,**

RANGE: throughout Arizona (Also: CA, NV, UT, CO, NM)

HABITAT: a wide variety of open areas from deserts to high mountains, gardens

SIMILAR SPECIES: See **American Lady** (page 180).

Admirals and Relatives ♦ Subfamily Limenitidinae

Red Admiral ♦ *Vanessa atalanta* 187a, b

KEY FIELD MARKS: *upf* (**187a**) **red-orange** median band on black; *uph* **red-orange** marginal outer band; *unf* (**187b**) blue circle with dark center between red-orange median band and outer white rectangle.

SIZE: 1$\frac{1}{2}$–2$\frac{1}{2}$ inches

ADULTS FLY: all year, weather permitting

HOST PLANTS: **nettle, pellitory**

RANGE: throughout Arizona except the extreme southwest (Also: CA, NV, UT, CO, NM)

HABITAT: a wide variety of open areas, streams, rivers

Mourning Cloak ♦ *Nymphalis antiopa* 189a, b

KEY FIELD MARKS: *ups* (189a) dark purple-black with submarginal **blue spots** and a wide **yellowish** marginal band; *uns* (189b) dark brown with a wide whitish marginal band.

SIZE: $2^5/_8$–$3^3/_8$

ADULTS FLY: January to mid-November, weather permitting

HOST PLANTS: **willows, quaking aspen**

RANGE: throughout Arizona except the extreme southwest (Also: CA, NV, UT, CO, NM)

HABITAT: streams, rivers, openings in many types of woodland

Common Buckeye ♦ *Junonia coenia* 191a, b

KEY FIELD MARKS: *uph* (**191a**) two postmedian circles contrasting in size; *upf* larger outer circle has **white border** that flares outward to the costa; *unh* (**191b**) tan with outline of circles showing through.

SIZE: 1³/₈–2¹/₄ inches

ADULTS FLY: all year, weather permitting

HOST PLANTS: **plaintains; toad flax, owl's clover, speedwells, frog fruit**

RANGE: throughout Arizona (Also: CA, NV, UT, CO, NM)

HABITAT: a wide variety of open areas

NOTES: Adults live about ten days. The white around the large *fw* eyespot is ultra violet reflecting. The senior author has seen individuals with all the large eyespot areas of the wings torn out, but the butterflies were still able to fly.

Tropical Buckeye ◆ *Junonia genoveva nigrosuffusa* 193a, b

KEY FIELD MARKS: *ups* (193a) similar to **Common Buckeye** but ground color **black**; *upf* circle **lacks** white border; *unh* (193b) tan with **wide brown** post-median band.

SIZE: 1³/₄–2³/₈ inches

ADULTS FLY: March to early January

HOST PLANTS: **monkeyflower, speedwell**

RANGE: throughout Arizona except the northeast one-third (Also: CA, NV, UT, CO, NM)

HABITAT: a wide variety of open areas

Admirals and Relatives ◆ Subfamily Limenitidinae

Red-spotted Admiral ◆ *Limenitus arthemis arizonensis* 195a, b

KEY FIELD MARKS: *ups* (**195a**) iridescent blue with a row of **light** submarginal spots; *uns* (**195b**) orange submarginal spots and red-orange post basal spots.

SIZE: $2^1/_2$–$3^5/_8$ inches

ADULTS FLY: late March to mid-November

HOST PLANTS: **willows, cottonwood, quaking aspen, chokecherry**

RANGE: throughout Arizona except the western one-quarter and the northeast (Also: NM)

HABITAT: streams and rivers in oak woodlands and mixed evergreen forests

SIMILAR SPECIES: **Pipevine Swallowtail** (page 22) has only **one row** of *unh* orange spots and has *hw* tails; *uph* has smaller spots not as near the edge.

NOTE: The **Red-spotted Admiral**, formerly called **Red-spotted Purple**, is a Batesian mimic of the **Pipevine Swallowtail**.

Viceroy ♦ *Limenitus archippus* 197a, b

KEY FIELD MARKS: *upf* (**197a**) four white postmedian spots; *uph* a row of post-median white spots; *unh* (**197b**) a black postmedian line bordering a row of white spots.

SIZE: $2^1/_4$–3 inches

ADULTS FLY: mid-April to mid-November

HOST PLANTS: **willow, Fremont cottonwood, quaking aspen**

RANGE: throughout Arizona except the extreme southwest, northeast and central-east (Also: CA, NV, UT, CO, NM)

HABITAT: near streams and rivers in a wide variety of habitats

SIMILAR SPECIES: **Monarch** (page 224), **Queen** (page 226) and **Soldier** (page 228) do not have *hw* postmedian black line with white spots.

Weidemeyer's Admiral ♦ *Limenitis weidemeyerii* 199a, b

KEY FIELD MARKS: *ups* (**199a**) black with a **wide white** postmedian band; *unh* (**199b**) with a wide **white** postmedian band, an **orange** submarginal band and a **white** marginal band.

SIZE: 2–3 inches

ADULTS FLY: mid-June to late July

HOST PLANTS: **willow, quaking aspen; chokecherry, service berry, rock spirea**

RANGE: roughly the northeastern half of Arizona including the extreme northwest (Also: CA, NV, UT, CO, NM)

HABITAT: streams, aspen groves and open woodland

NOTE: The white *ups* areas reflect ultraviolet light while the black absorbs it.

California Sister ♦ *Adelpha bredowii* 201a, b

KEY FIELD MARKS: *ups* (**201a**) **white** postmedial band; *upf* **orange** patch at sub-apex; *uns* (**201b**) blue, orange and white pattern.

SIZE: $2^1/_4$–3 inches

ADULTS FLY: early April to early December

HOST PLANTS: various "evergreen" **oaks, Gambel's oak**

RANGE: throughout Arizona except the low desert of the southwest and south-central (Also: CA, NV, UT, CO, NM)

HABITAT: oak woodland, streams in foothills and mountains

NOTE: The white band reflects ultraviolet light and the black absorbs it.

Common Mestra ♦ *Mestra amymone* 203a, b

KEY FIELD MARKS: *uph* (**203a**) wide **pale apricot** marginal band; *unh* (**203b**) pale apricot with white median band and grayish inner band.

SIZE: $1^3/_8$–$1^3/_4$ inches

ADULTS FLY: early August to mid-November; a rare monsoon influx species that occasionally breeds in the state

HOST PLANTS: **nose burn**

RANGE: southeastern Arizona and one Coconino County record (Also: NM)

HABITAT: streams and woodland edges

Ruddy Daggerwing ♦ *Marpesia petreus* 205a, b

KEY FIELD MARKS: *ups* (**205a**) **bright orange** with narrow black lines, *fw* apex squared off, *hw* with long **tails**; *uns* (**205b**) brown with narrow darker median band.

SIZE: $2^{1}/_{2}$–$3^{3}/_{8}$ inches

ADULTS FLY: early August to mid-October as a rare monsoon influx species (but see Note)

HOST PLANT: **figs**

RANGE: southeastern Arizona (Also: NM, CO)

HABITAT: mesquite forests and edges

NOTE: In the summer of 1983, this species invaded the state in large numbers and is thought to have bred on introduced figs.

Leafwings ♦ Subfamily Charaxinae

Tropical Leafwing ♦ *Anaea aidea* 207a

KEY FIELD MARKS: *ups* orange; *uns* gray with a tail on *hw* with a **smaller protuberance** under the tail.

SIZE: $2^1/_4$–$2^1/_2$ inches

ADULTS FLY: mid-March to late June and early August to mid- December (at least two broods)

HOST PLANTS: **croton** species suspected

RANGE: southeastern Arizona (Also: NM)

HABITAT: foothill streams

SIMILAR SPECIES: **Goatweed Leafwing** lacks small protuberance under the tail.

Goatweed Leafwing ♦ *Anaea andria* 207b

KEY FIELD MARKS: *ups* orange; *uns* tail on *hw*, *fw* apex falcate.

SIZE: $1^3/_4$–$2^7/_8$

ADULTS FLY: mid-February to mid-May and early July to mid-October (two broods)

HOST PLANT: **Texas croton**

RANGE: roughly central to southeastern Arizona (Also: CO, NM)

HABITAT: open areas along streams and washes

Emperors ◆ Subfamily Apaturinae

Hackberry Emperor ◆ *Asterocampa celtis* 209a

KEY FIELD MARKS: *upf* **three brown innermost spots** on basal portion near costa; *unf* (**209a**) **three** brown spots on basal portion near costa, top eyespot with **white center**.

SIZE: 1^1/$_2$–2^1/$_4$ inches

ADULTS FLY: late April to late October

HOST PLANT: **netleaf hackberry**

RANGE: roughly northwest through the center of Arizona to the southeast (Also: NV, UT, CO, NM)

HABITAT: watercourses with host plant

SIMILAR SPECIES: **Empress Leilia** and **Tawny Emperor** (page 210) have only two *fw* rectangles near base; top *unf* eyespot of **Empress Leilia** blue center while **Tawny Emperor** lacks eyespots on *fw*.

Empress Leilia ◆ *Asterocampa leilia* 209b, c

KEY FIELD MARKS: *upf* (**209b**) **two** brown innermost rectangles along costa; *unf* (**209c**) top eyespot has **blue center, whitish** between two innermost brown rectangles.

SIZE: 1^1/$_2$–2 inches

ADULTS FLY: late February to mid-December

HOST PLANT: **desert hackberry**

RANGE: roughly central and southern Arizona except for the southwest (Also: NM)

HABITAT: desert washes and scrub

SIMILAR SPECIES: See **Hackberry Emperor**.

Tawny Emperor ♦ *Asterocampa clyton* **211a, b**

KEY FIELD MARKS: *upf* (**211a**) similar to Empress Leilia but **no eyespots**; *unf* (**211b**) a white median band, two innermost costal spots, **no eyespots**.

SIZE: 1⅝–2½ inches

ADULTS FLY: late April to late October (two to three broods)

HOST PLANT: **netleaf hackberry**

RANGE: southeastern Arizona (Also: NM)

HABITAT: canyons and washes near food plant

SIMILAR SPECIES: See **Hackberry Emperor** (page 208).

Satyrs ◆ Subfamily Satyrinae

Nabokov's Satyr ◆ *Cyllopsis pyracmon* 213a

KEY FIELD MARKS: *unh* straight postmedian band connects to the **top** of the wing, two iridescent eyespots on the outer margin.

SIZE: $1^1/_2$–$1^3/_4$ inches

ADULTS FLY: early April to mid-October

HOST PLANTS: **bullgrass** and other grasses

RANGE: southeast Arizona (Also: NM)

HABITAT: oak and pine woodland

SIMILAR SPECIES: **Canyonland Satyr** *unh* postmedian band **curves outward**.

Canyonland Satyr ◆ *Cyllopsis pertepida* 213b

KEY FIELD MARKS: *unh* postmedian band **curves outward** and does not reach the top of the wing, two iridescent eye spots on the outer margin.

SIZE: $1^1/_4$–$1^5/_8$ inches

ADULTS FLY: late May to late July and mid-September to mid- November (two broods)

HOST PLANTS: not known—probably grasses

RANGE: throughout Arizona except for the southwestern quarter (Also: NV, UT, CO, NM)

HABITAT: upland canyons, ravines

Small Wood-Nymph ◆ *Cercyonis oetus* 213c

KEY FIELD MARKS: *unf* lower eyespot **much smaller** (or absent) than the upper; *unh* **zigzag dark lines** (especially inner one).

SIZE: $1^1/_4$–$1^3/_4$ inches

ADULTS FLY: late June through August

HOST PLANTS: not known—probably grasses

RANGE: across the northern border of Arizona through the northeast corner and down the eastern border to the White Mountains (Also: CA, NV UT, CO, NM)

HABITAT: pine woodland, sagebrush

SIMILAR SPECIES: **Common** (page 216) and **Great Basin Wood Nymph** (page 216) **lack** *unh* zigzag dark lines.

Pine Satyr ♦ *Paramacera allyni* 215a

KEY FIELD MARKS: *unh* six submarginal eyespots with **white centers**, dark base, wide tan median band; *unf* one large eyespot at sub-apex.

SIZE: 1^1/$_4$–1^3/$_4$ inches

ADULTS FLY: late May to mid-August

HOST PLANTS: not known—probably grasses

RANGE: southeastern Arizona (Huachuca and Chiricahua Mountains)

HABITAT: coniferous forest

SIMILAR SPECIES: See **Red Satyr.**

Red Satyr ♦ *Megisto rubricata* 215b, c

KEY FIELD MARKS: *ups* (**215b**) large reddish patches in outer portions; *unh* (**215c**) **two** large eyespots and smaller blue eyespots outside narrow postmedian band; *unf* large eyespot at sub-apex, when wing is raised, **red is seen.**

SIZE: 1^3/$_8$–1^7/$_8$ inches

ADULTS FLY: mid-May to mid-November

HOST PLANTS: grasses (oviposition observed on **crinkle awn**—Bailowitz and Brock 1991)

RANGE: central through the southeastern quarter of Arizona (Also: NM)

HABITAT: oak woodland, mesquite

SIMILAR SPECIES: **Common** (page 216), **Great Basin** (page 216) and **Small Wood Nymph** (page 212) lack red in *fw*. **Pine Satyr** has more *hw* eyespots with white centers.

Great Basin Wood-Nymph ♦ *Cercyonis sthenele* 217a

KEY FIELD MARKS: *uns* no contrast between basal and distal portions, postmedian submarginal eyespots with white centers; *unf* lower eyespot smaller than upper eyespot.

SIZE: 1$\frac{3}{8}$–1$\frac{5}{8}$ inches

ADULTS FLY: late June to early August

HOST PLANTS: grasses

RANGE: along the northern border of Arizona (Also: CA, NV, UT, CO, NM)

HABITAT: pinyon-juniper woodland

SIMILAR SPECIES: **Common Wood Nymph:** *uns* outer half has contrast with slightly darker inner half; *unf* lower eyespot usually equal to or slightly larger than upper. **Mead's Wood Nymph** has orange between the two *unf* eyespots. **Small Wood Nymph** (page 212) has zigzag dark lines in *unh*.

Common Wood-Nymph ♦ *Cercyonis pegala* 217b

KEY FIELD MARKS: *uns* basal half darker than outer half; *unf* lower eyespot as big or slightly larger than top eyespot.

SIZE: 1$\frac{7}{8}$–2$\frac{5}{8}$ inches

ADULTS FLY: late June through early July

HOST PLANTS: **wild oat**, several species of *Andropogon*

RANGE: north-central to east-central along the Mogollon Rim of Arizona (Also: CA, NV, UT, CO, NM)

HABITAT: grassland

SIMILAR SPECIES: See **Great Basin Wood Nymph.**

Mead's Wood-Nymph ♦ *Cercyonis meadii* 217c

KEY FIELD MARKS: *unf* light orange between the two eyespots

SIZE: 1$\frac{1}{2}$–1$\frac{5}{8}$ inches

ADULTS FLY: late June to early September

HOST PLANTS: grasses

RANGE: roughly north of a line drawn from the northwest corner to the southeast corner of Arizona (Also: UT, CO, NM)

SIMILAR SPECIES: **Red Satyr** (page 214) has two *unh* eyespots with white centers.

Red-bordered Satyr ◆ *Gyrocheilus patrobas* 219a, b

KEY FIELD MARKS: *fw* (**219a**) **four submarginal white dots;** *hw* (**219b**) wide **red marginal** band.

SIZE: 2-2$\frac{1}{4}$ inches

ADULTS FLY: mid-August to early November

HOST PLANT: **bull grass**

RANGE: central to central-eastern and southeastern Arizona (Also: NM)

HABITAT: mountains

Common Ringlet ♦ *Coenonympha tullia* 221a

KEY FIELD MARKS: *unf* orangish-brown, **large eyespot** with white center near sub-apex; *unh* gray with **dark-centered** submarginal eyespots.

SIZE: 1–1$^1/_4$ inches

ADULTS FLY: June through August

HOST PLANTS: grasses

RANGE: two disjunct populations, one on the South Rim of the Grand Canyon and the other in the White Mountains in the east (Jim Brock—*pers. comm.*) (Also: CA, NV, UT, CO, NM)

HABITAT: open grasslands in a variety of areas

Alberta Arctic ♦ *Oeneis alberta daura* 221b

KEY FIELD MARKS: *unh* mottled brown with indistinct black median band.

SIZE: 1$^1/_4$–1$^5/_8$ inches

ADULTS FLY: May through June

HOST PLANTS: **bunchgrass, fescue**

RANGE: two disjunct populations one in the San Francisco Peaks area and the other in the White Mountains (Jim Brock—*pers. comm.*) (Also: CO, NM)

HABITAT: high mountain grasslands

SIMILAR SPECIES: **Wood-Nymphs** and **Satyrs** have eyespots.

Ridings' Satyr ◆ *Neominois ridingsii* 223a, b

KEY FIELD MARKS: *unf* (**223b**) has black eyespot with whitish border extending outwardly as two acute prongs; *ups* (**223a**) postmedian to submarginal band of **elongated white ovals**.

SIZE: 1³/₈–2 inches

ADULTS FLY: mid-June to early August

HOST PLANT: **blue grama**

RANGE: northwestern extending into the north-central part of Arizona; also the White Mountains in the east (Also: CA, NV, UT, CO, NM)

HABITAT: grassland, sagebrush

SIMILAR SPECIES: **Alberta Arctic** (page 220) lacks *fw* eyespot.

Monarchs ♦ Subfamily Danainae

Monarch ♦ *Danaus plexippus* 225a, b

KEY FIELD MARKS: *upf* (**225a**) black apex with white spots, sub-apex with orangish spots in black; *unf* (**225b**) black with white spots and yellow ovals in outer portion; *unh* yellow with black veins and marginal black border with white spots.

SIZE: 3–4$^1/_2$ inches

ADULTS FLY: late summer and early fall

HOST PLANTS: **milkweed** species

RANGE: throughout Arizona (Also: CA, NV, UT, CO, NM)

HABITAT: a wide variety of open areas

SIMILAR SPECIES: **Queen** (page 226) and **Soldier** (page 228) lack *fw* dark sub-apex.

Queen ♦ *Danaus gilippus* 227a, b

KEY FIELD MARKS: *fw* two rows of white spots in orange.

SIZE: 2³/₄–3¹/₂ inches

ADULTS FLY: all year, weather permitting

HOST PLANTS: many **milkweed** Species

RANGE: throughout Arizona (Also: CA, NV, UT, CO, NM)

HABITAT: a wide variety of open areas

SIMILAR SPECIES: **Viceroy** (page 196): *hw* has black postmedian line. **Monarch** (page 224) has dark *fw* sub-apex. **Soldier** (page 228) lacks a complete inner row of white *fw* spots but has an irregular brown *unh* band.

Soldier ◆ *Danaus eresimus* 229a, b

KEY FIELD MARKS: *fw* (**229a**) has two rows of spots (inner row short, does not cross into orange); *unh* (**229b**) **splashes of white** around black veins and an **irregular** brown median band.

SIZE: $2^1/_2$–$3^1/_2$ inches

ADULTS FLY: a rare monsoon influx species—mid-August to mid-November

HOST PLANTS: **milkweeds**

RANGE: southeastern Arizona (also: NM)

HABITAT: open grasslands, riparian, wooded edges

SIMILAR SPECIES: **Viceroy** (page 196): *hw* has a black postmedian line. **Queen** (page 226) has a complete row of white spots on outer *fw*. **Monarch** (page 224) has dark *fw* apex.

NOTE: The **Soldier** is a Mullerian mimic with the **Monarch**, **Queen** and **Viceroy**.

Skippers ♦ *Family Hesperiidae*

We follow the **North American Butterfly Association**'s classification that divides the Skippers into five subfamilies:

Of the 272 species of Skippers in North America, 137 (50%) occur in Arizona. Skippers differ from other butterflies by having the tips of their antennae clubs hooked backward, stocky bodies, strong wing muscles and better eyes.

To be a Skipper observer takes keen attention. It also takes an attitude adjustment to get started. Just as the amateur botanist may leave grasses or sunflowers until later, or a beginning birder will balk when it comes to learning the plumages of gulls, so the beginning butterflyer may not attempt to distinguish the Skippers at first. Reasons are that they are small, brown and difficult to follow and that many species, especially within the same genus, superficially look alike. In fact, some species in the genera *Erynnis*, *Hesperia* and *Amblyscirtes* cannot be told apart in the field even by experts (but start with the **Dull Firetip**, *Pyrrhopyge araxes*—a large easily identified species—on the opposite page). This is especially true if the butterflies are even a little worn.

We remember that 30 years ago experts were telling us that Empidonax flycatchers were only identifiable in the hand. It is still difficult to identify these flycatchers in the field, but birders have discovered ways to do it. In the meantime, we accept that it is valuable to collect butterflies in order to know exactly what species is being studied.

Skipper watching sometimes takes total concentration. We find that it is a great pleasure to be in the field with a camera trying to photograph these elusive creatures. All insect movement is intriguing. Because Skippers are so fascinating to us, we watch *all motion*. Flying insects, including Skippers, usually end up landing. One has to mentally mark exactly *where* they have landed. Otherwise, their natural camouflage makes them almost invisible. Skippers are the ultimate challenge for butterfly watchers. As you can see from these photographs, they have a beauty that you do not want to miss.

Dull Firetip *Pyrrhopyge araxes* **231**

Dull Firetip ♦ *Pyrrhopyge araxes* 231, 233a

KEY FIELD MARKS: *fw* (**231**) three groups of three silvery rectangles; *unh* (**233a**) yellowish-orange with black outer margin, white fringe checkered with black.

SIZE: $1^3/_4$–$2^3/_8$ inches

ADULTS FLY: mid-July to mid-October

HOST PLANT: **Arizona white oak** and other oaks

RANGE: southeast Arizona (also: NM)

HABITAT: oak woodland and riparian in oak woodland

Silver-spotted Skipper ♦ *Epargyreus clarus* 233b, c

KEY FIELD MARKS: *unh* (**233c**) large median **silver patch**; *upf* (**233b**) **gold median band** composed of four different-sized rectangles.

SIZE: $1^5/_8$–$1^7/_8$ inches

ADULTS FLY: mid-April to late September

HOST PLANTS: **New Mexican locust, bastard indigo, licorice**

RANGE: throughout Arizona except the southwestern quarter and extreme north central (Also: CA, NV, UT, CO, NM)

HABITAT: riparian, mountain canyons

SIMILAR SPECIES: **Wind's Silverdrop** (page 372), a very rare stray, has frosted outer *fw*.

NOTE: This is the beginning of the **Speadwing Skippers**, which land and often perch with their wings flat (but Cloudywings hold their wings only partially open). Their host plants are various herbs, bushes and trees. The other big sub-family, the **Skipperlings** and **Grass Skippers**, start on page 268. These Skippers are smaller, mostly orangish or brown, and while perched often hold their front wings at a 45-degree angle and their hind wings at a 90-degree angle from the body. Fortunately, they also close both wings often so that one can view the *unh* pattern.

Hammock Skipper ♦ *Polygonus leo* 233d

KEY FIELD MARKS: *fw* **three large rectangular spots**, top spot with indented outer edge; *unh* **short tail**, two brown bands, violet glaze.

SIZE: $1^3/_4$–2 inches

ADULTS FLY: mid-July to late October as strays

HOST PLANTS: not known in Arizona—probably does not breed in the state

RANGE: has been found from the western through the central and southern to the southeastern portions of Arizona (Also: CA, NV, UT, NM)

HABITAT: riparian

White-striped Longtail ◆ *Chioides catillus albofasciatus* 235a

KEY FIELD MARKS: *unh* has a prominent **diagonal white stripe**.

SIZE: 1^3/$_4$–2 inches

ADULTS FLY: early March to early December

HOST PLANTS: not known in state but several viney bean species are possible

RANGE: extreme southeast Arizona (Also: NM)

HABITAT: dry canyons

Zilpa Longtail ◆ *Chioides zilpa* 235b

KEY FIELD MARKS: *unh* large **white patch** on trailing edge, four large dark **brown spots** on basal half.

SIZE: 1^7/$_8$–2^1/$_4$ inches

ADULTS FLY: as a rare monsoon vagrant from late August to late October

HOST PLANTS: not known to breed in the state

RANGE: extreme southeast Arizona

HABITAT: found in many types as a stray

SIMILAR SPECIES: **White-striped Longtail** has a prominent diagonal white stripe traversing the *unh*.

Short-tailed Skipper ♦ *Zestusa dorus* 237a, b

KEY FIELD MARKS: *upf* (**237a**) three **white** rectangles on outer costa, three gold median spots and four gold postmedian spots; *hw* (**237b**) **short tail**; *unh* narrow **black** median band, black rectangular spot with **white patch** at corner.

SIZE: $1^1/_2$–$1^5/_8$ inches

ADULTS FLY: early July to early September; an additional spring flight in southeastern Arizona mid-March to early May

HOST PLANTS: **Emory**, **Arizona** and **Gambel Oak**

RANGE: roughly throughout Arizona except the southwest one-third (Also: UT, CO, NM)

HABITAT: oak woodland

SIMILAR SPECIES: The short tail and white on both wings are unique.

Arizona Skipper ♦ *Codatractus arizonensis* 237c

KEY FIELD MARKS: *unf* **wide** silvery median band, four smaller silvery rectangles on outer costa; *unh* wide **white marginal band** containing a submarginal **brown band** on the outer edge.

SIZE: $1^5/_8$–$2^{15}/_{16}$ inches

ADULTS FLY: late March to mid-October

HOST PLANT: **kidney wood**

RANGE: extreme southeastern Arizona (Also: NM)

HABITAT: mountain canyons

SIMILAR SPECIES: **Desert Cloudywing** has **thin brownish vertical streaks** in the *unh* white marginal band, and the *unf* median spots along the costa are smaller.

Desert Cloudywing ♦ *Achalarus casica* 237d

KEY FIELD MARKS: *unh* white marginal band as **thin brownish** vertical streaks.

SIZE: $1^1/_2$–2 inches

ADULTS FLY: late April to early October

HOST PLANTS: **tick clover**, **butterfly pea**

RANGE: extreme southeast Arizona (Also: NM)

HABITAT: pinyon-juniper and oak woodlands, mountain canyons

Long-tailed Skipper ♦ *Urbanus proteus* 239a, b

KEY FIELD MARKS: *ups* (239a) top of head, thorax and base of wings **iridescent green-blue**; *upf* four median rectangular spots; *unh* (239b) inner brown band with two spots above; *unf* dark brown submarginal band **not broken**.

SIZE: 1¹/₂–2 inches

ADULTS FLY: as stray and occasional breeder—records in April and May, but most seen early August to mid-November

HOST PLANTS: **tick clovers, butterfly pea, mesquite**

RANGE: southern Arizona (Also: CA, NM)

HABITAT: open brushy areas, gardens, many habitats as a stray

SIMILAR SPECIES: **Dorantes Longtail** lacks *ups* iridescence.

Dorantes Longtail ♦ *Urbanus dorantes* 239c, d

KEY FIELD MARKS: *ups* (239c) thorax brown; *upf* similar to **Long-tailed Skipper**; *unh* (239d) similar to **Long-tailed Skipper**; *unf* submarginal dark band **broken** near sub-apex.

SIZE: 1¹/₂–2 inches

ADULTS FLY: mid-July to late November

HOST PLANTS: **tick clovers**

RANGE: southern Arizona (Also: NM)

HABITAT: foothill canyons and gardens

SIMILAR SPECIES: **Long-tailed Skipper** has *ups* iridescent green-blue on thorax, top of head, and base of wings.

Golden Banded-Skipper ♦ *Autochton cellus* 241

KEY FIELD MARKS: *upf* prominent **gold median band** with three small silvery spots near subapex.

SIZE: 1$\frac{1}{4}$–1$\frac{3}{4}$ inches

ADULTS FLY: mid-June to early September

HOST PLANTS: **New Mexican locust, butterfly pea, beans**

RANGE: central east to southeast Arizona (Also: NM)

HABITAT: canyon riparian

Northern Cloudywing ♦ *Thorybes pylades* 243a, b

KEY FIELD MARKS: *fw* usually has a triangle of postmedian spots (but can have more than three); *hw* **brown** margin.

SIZE: 1¼–1½ inches

ADULTS FLY: late April to early September

HOST PLANTS: **narrowleaf tick clover, tick seed, stinking willow, alfalfa, rosary bean, clovers, American vetch**

RANGE: roughly throughout Arizona except the southwest quarter (Also: CA, NV, UT, CO, NM)

HABITAT: woodlands, canyons, streams

SIMILAR SPECIES: **Mexican Cloudywing** has *unh* outer edge paler with fine short striations. **Drusius Cloudywing** (page 244) has white fringe on *hw* margin.

Mexican Cloudywing ♦ *Thorybes mexicanus dobra* 243c, d

KEY FIELD MARKS: *upf* (**243c**) middle postmedian spots include an **inner elongated spot**; *unh* (243d) **paler** outer half with **short fine striations**.

SIZE: 1–1½ inches

ADULTS FLY: late April to early July

HOST PLANTS: **American vetch, clover, mountain pea**

RANGE: throughout the eastern mountains of Arizona (Also: CA, NV, UT, CO, NM)

HABITAT: meadows, streams, rocky areas

SIMILAR SPECIES: See **Northern Cloudywing**.

Drusius Cloudywing ♦ *Thorybes drusius* 245a, b

KEY FIELD MARKS: *fw* very similar to **Northern Cloudywing**; *hw* white fringe.

SIZE: 1¹/₂ inches

ADULTS FLY: July to late August

HOST PLANT: *Cologania*

RANGE: extreme southeastern Arizona (Also: NM)

HABITAT: riparian, grassland, oak woodland

SIMILAR SPECIES: See **Northern Cloudywing** (page 242).

Acacia Skipper ♦ *Cogia hippalus* 245c

KEY FIELD MARKS: *unf* median band of spots narrow; *unh* two brown bands with white margin and fringe.

SIZE: 1¹/₄–1⁷/₈ inches

ADULTS FLY: mid-March to mid-October

HOST PLANT: **white ball acacia**

RANGE: central through southeastern Arizona (Also: NM)

HABITAT: desert grassland, pinyon-juniper woodland

SIMILAR SPECIES: **Gold-costa Skipper** has a **gold costa**. **Arizona Skipper** (page 236) and **Desert Cloudywing** (page 236) have a wider *unh* white marginal band.

Gold-costa Skipper ♦ *Cogia caicus* 245d

KEY FIELD MARKS: *fw* gold costa.

SIZE: 1–1¹/₂ inches

ADULTS FLY: mid-March to late May and mid-July to early September (two broods)

HOST PLANT: **white ball acacia**

RANGE: roughly central through southeastern Arizona (Also: NM)

HABITAT: oak-pine woodland

NOTE: formerly called **Caicus Skipper**

Golden-headed Scallopwing ♦ *Staphylus ceos* 247a

KEY FIELD MARKS: **Golden head and palps** (in a very few individuals these are black). Almost always perches with wings flat.

SIZE: 3/4–1 inch

ADULTS FLY: early February to mid-November

HOST PLANT: **Fremont's goosefoot**

RANGE: central to southeastern Arizona (Also: NM)

HABITAT: desert flats and washes

SIMILAR SPECIES: **Orange-edged Roadside-Skipper** (page 318) has **orange** fringes. **Orange-headed Roadside-Skipper** (page 320) has **white** fringes. Neither has orange palps, nor do they ever perch with wings flat.

Texas Powdered-Skipper ♦ *Systasea pulverulenta* 247b

KEY FIELD MARKS: *upf* silvery median band has **straight inner edge;** *hw* scalloped margin.

SIZE: 1–1 1/4 inches

ADULTS FLY: early August to mid-November

HOST PLANTS: **Indian mallow, globe mallow**

RANGE: extreme southeastern Arizona in Santa Cruz County (Also: NM)

HABITAT: riparian washes, open woods

SIMILAR SPECIES: See **Arizona Powdered Skipper.**

Arizona Powdered-Skipper ♦ *Systasea zampa* 247c

KEY FIELD MARKS: *upf* silvery median band is **offset;** *hw* scalloped margin

SIZE: 1–1 1/2 inches

ADULTS FLY: all year, weather permitting

HOST PLANTS: several **Indian mallows,** *Herissantia*

RANGE: central west to southwest (except the Yuma area) across to southeastern Arizona (Also: CA, NV, NM)

HABITAT: dry canyons, washes

SIMILAR SPECIES: **Texas Powdered Skipper** has a **straight inner edge** to the silvery median band.

White-patched Skipper ♦ *Chiomara asychis georgina* 249a

KEY FIELD MARKS: *uph* large median **white patch**; *upf* irregular white median band.

SIZE: 1–1³/₈ inches

ADULTS FLY: records for most of the year

HOST PLANTS: not known in state—but **Malpighia** family suspected

RANGE: extreme southeastern Arizona (Also: NM)

HABITAT: woodland edges, gardens

Brown-banded Skipper ♦ *Timochares ruptifasciatus* 249b

KEY FIELD MARKS: *uph* **three dark** brown horizontal bands.

SIZE: 1¹/₂–1³/₄ inches

ADULTS FLY: September and October as a stray

HOST PLANT: not known in state

RANGE: extreme south of Arizona

HABITAT: woodland edges, gardens

Valeriana Skipper ♦ *Codatractus mysie* 249c

KEY FIELD MARKS: *unh* brown with **darker brown** median and postmedian bands.

SIZE: 1¹/₂–1⁷/₈ inches

ADULTS FLY: late July to late August

HOST PLANT: *Tephrosia leiocarpa*

RANGE: southeastern Arizona in Santa Cruz County

HABITAT: rocky canyons

Dreamy Duskywing ♦ *Erynnis icelus* 251a

KEY FIELD MARKS: **labial palpi projecting forward**; *upf* **chain-like** postmedian band with **whitish rectangle** just inside that band; *uph* pale dots on brown; *uns* tiny pale dots on brown.

SIZE: $7/8$–1 inch   ADULTS FLY: early June to early July

HOST PLANT: **quaking aspen**

RANGE: roughly the northeastern half of Arizona (Also: CA, NV, UT, CO, NM)

HABITAT: forest edges, streams, open woods

SIMILAR SPECIES: **Sleepy Duskywing**: usually no whitish rectangle inside post median band and if present not as large nor as gray; the **Dreamy** and the **Sleepy** are the only two species that have chain-like streaking on the *upf*. **Dreamy** is usually found only at elevations above 6,000 feet. **Sleepy Duskywing** occurs at **lower elevation and flies earlier**. All other Duskywings have many small glassine spots on the *fw* and the labial palpi do not project forward.

NOTE: Species in the genus *Erynnis* are notoriously difficult to differentiate in the field.

Sleepy Duskywing ♦ *Erynnis brizo burgessi* 251b, c

KEY FIELD MARKS: *upf* (**251b**) no white spots; postmedian band **usually without** whitish rectangle just inside the upper part of the band—but if present, not as large nor as gray as the one on **Dreamy Duskywing**; *uph* pale dots on brown; *uns* (**251c**) tiny pale dots on brown.

SIZE: $1 1/4$–$1 3/8$ inches   ADULTS FLY: early February to early May

HOST PLANTS: **Gambel's oak, wavy leaf oak, scrub oak**

RANGE: roughly throughout Arizona except southwestern quarter (Also: CA, NV, UT, CO, NM)

HABITAT: oak or pine-oak woodland, oak scrub

Juvenal's Duskywing ♦ *Erynnis juvenalis clitus* 251d

KEY FIELD MARKS: *upf* much **gray**, white spots large, pale spot just down from mid-costa (end of *fw* cell); *hw* white fringe; *unh* two round light subapical spots on leading edge.

SIZE: $1 1/4$–$1 1/2$ inches   ADULTS FLY: mid-March to early September

HOST PLANTS: **Arizona oak, Emory oak, gray oak**

RANGE: southeast corner of Arizona (Also: NM)

HABITAT: oak woodland

SIMILAR SPECIES: **Horace's Duskywing** (page 254): **mostly brown in *upf*** and lacks *hw* white fringe of Arizona race of **Juvenal's Duskywing**. **Rocky Mountain Duskywing** (page 252) also has much **gray** on *upf*. However, neither of these two species overlap range of **Juvenal's**. **Funereal Duskywing** (page 256) has a pale patch just inside the costal glassine spots on *upf*. **Mournful Duskywing** (page 254) has **additional inner white spots** just inside the white fringe on the *unh*.

Rocky Mountain Duskywing ♦ *Erynnis telemachus* 253a, b

KEY FIELD MARKS: *upf* (253a) mottled black and gray with glassine spots; *uph* brown with pale spots, fringe **pale but not bright white**; *unh* (253b) two small sub-apical pale spots along leading edge. **Female 253a**; **Male 253b**.

SIZE: 1¼–1⅝ inches

ADULTS FLY: mid-May to mid-July

HOST PLANT: **Gambel's oak**

RANGE: northern, central and eastern Arizona south through the Mogollon Rim and the White Mountains (Also: NV, UT, CO, NM)

HABITAT: oak and pine-oak woodland

SIMILAR SPECIES: Overlaps in White Mountains with **Juvenal's Duskywing** (page 250) which has a **brighter whiter fringe**. **Horace's Duskywing** (page 254) (overlaps only in the very extreme northeast corner) has **brown** *upf* and lacks two pale spots on **unh**.

Meridian Duskywing ♦ *Erynnis meridianus* no photo

KEY FIELD MARKS: *upf* with glassine spots; *hw* with **brown** fringe.

SIZE: 1¼–1⅝ inches

ADULTS FLY: mid-June to mid-September

HOST PLANT: **Arizona oak**

RANGE: from northwest corner through central part of Arizona to the southeast (Also: NV, UT, NM)

HABITAT: oak woodland

SIMILAR SPECIES: **Juvenal's Duskywing** (page 250) has *hw* white fringe; can be differentiated reliably from **Horace's Duskywing** (page 254) only by the male genitalia.

Scudder's Duskywing ♦ *Erynnis scudderi* no photo

KEY FIELD MARKS: *upf* has translucent white spots, male has dense covering of long brown hairlike scales; *hw* **white** fringe.

SIZE: 1⅛–1½ inches

ADULTS FLY: mid-April to early September

HOST PLANTS: not known but probably oaks

RANGE: southeastern corner of Arizona (Also: NM)

HABITAT: oak woodland

SIMILAR SPECIES: Can reliably be differentiated from **Juvenal's** (page 250) and **Pacuvius** (page 254) **Duskywings** only by examining the male genitalia.

Horace's Duskywing ♦ *Erynnis horatius* (Spring Form) 255a, b

KEY FIELD MARKS: *upf* (255a) **mostly brown**, white spots large, white spot just down from mid-costa (end of *fw* cell); *hw* (255b) fringe pale (not white); **white line over eye**.

SIZE: 1¼–1¾ inches

ADULTS FLY: April through August

HOST PLANT: **Gambel's oak**

RANGE: extreme northeastern Arizona (Also: UT, CO, NM)

HABITAT: oak woodland

SIMILAR SPECIES: See **Juvenal's Duskywing**.

Mournful Duskywing ♦ *Erynnis tristis* 255c

KEY FIELD MARKS: *upf* gray with several glassine white spots; *hw* white fringe; *unh* **white spots just inside the fringe**.

SIZE: 1⅛–1¾ inches

ADULTS FLY: late February to late October

HOST PLANTS: oaks used elsewhere—probably in Arizona also

RANGE: roughly from central northwest through center of Arizona to the southeast (Also: CA, NV, UT, CO, NM)

HABITAT: oak woodland

SIMILAR SPECIES: See **Juvenal's Duskywing** (page 250).

Pacuvius Duskywing ♦ *Erynnis pacuvius* 255d

KEY FIELD MARKS: *upf* brown with many tan patches; *hw* with **white fringe**.

SIZE: 1–1¼ inches

ADULTS FLY: late March to late October (at least two broods)

HOST PLANT: **Fendler ceanothus**

RANGE: roughly north central through eastern half of Arizona (Also: CA, NV, UT, CO, NM)

HABITAT: chaparral and mixed woodlands with food plant

SIMILAR SPECIES: **Persius Duskywing** (page 258) has a brown fringe, shorter, rounder wings, lesser contrasting *ups* colors. **Afranius Duskywing** (page 256) has a pale fringe, less contrasting *ups* colors. **Juvenal's** (page 250), **Scudder's** (page 252) and **Funeral** (page 256) **Duskywings** have less contrasting *ups* colors. **Mournful Duskywing** has *unh* white spots inside of the fringe.

Funereal Duskywing ♦ *Erynnis funeralis* 257a, b

KEY FIELD MARKS: *upf* (257a) dark with a **pale patch** just inside the four white sub-apical spots; *uph* dark with **white fringe**.

SIZE: 1^1/$_4$–1^1/$_2$ inches

ADULTS FLY: all year, weather permitting

HOST PLANTS: **New Mexican locust, butterfly pea, alfalfa, Galactica**

RANGE: throughout Arizona (Also: CA, NV, UT, CO, NM)

HABITAT: a wide variety from desert washes and open flats to oak woodlands

SIMILAR SPECIES: Other white-fringed Duskywings lack the pale patch on the *fw*.

Afranius Duskywing ♦ *Erynnis afranius* 257c, d

KEY FIELD MARKS: *upf* brownish-black with tan patch just inward from white apical spots; *hw* pale fringe. **Male 257c**; female **257d**.

SIZE: ^{7}/$_8$–1^1/$_4$ inches

ADULTS FLY: May to mid-August

HOST PLANTS: **lupine, Spanish clover**

RANGE: throughout except roughly southwest one-third of Arizona

HABITAT: meadows, streams, woodlands

SIMILAR SPECIES: See **Persius Duskywing** (page 258).

Mountain Checkered-Skipper ♦ *Pyrgus xanthus* 259a

KEY FIELD MARKS: *upf* has no spots immediately outside the median white rectangular costal spot; *uph* white fringe with **black** streaks that **extend to the edge** of fringe.

SIZE: $3/4$–1 inch

ADULTS FLY: May and June

HOST PLANTS: several species of **cinquefoil**

RANGE: along the east central border and north central area of Arizona (Also: UT, CO, NM)

HABITAT: forest openings, grasslands

SIMILAR SPECIES: **Common** (page 260) and **White Checkered-Skippers** (page 260) (**Desert** and **Tropical** do not overlap) *upf* have **more** white spots and **small distinct white submarginal spots. Small Checkered-Skipper** has white fringe with black streaks that extend **only halfway** to the edge.

Small Checkered-Skipper ♦ *Pyrgus scriptura* 259b

KEY FIELD MARKS: similar to **Mountain Checkered-Skipper** but **black** streaks in *uph* white fringe extend only **halfway** to edge.

SIZE: $5/8$–$7/8$ inch

ADULTS FLY: February through October

HOST PLANTS: **alkali mallow, globe mallow, apricot mallow**

RANGE: throughout Arizona except central portion and along the southwest to south central border (Also: CA, NV, UT, CO, NM)

HABITAT: flats, agricultural areas, open areas with bare places; usually at lower elevation than **Mountain Checkered-Skipper**

Persius Duskywing ♦ *Erynnis persius* 259c

KEY FIELD MARKS: *ups* mottled gray and brown with glassine spots; *upf* males have numerous white hairs; *hw* brown fringe.

SIZE: $7/8$–$1 3/8$ inches

ADULTS FLY: late April to early July

HOST PLANTS: **golden pea, lupines, quaking aspen**

RANGE: throughout Arizona except for roughly the southwestern one third (Also: CA, NV, UT, NM)

HABITAT: mountain meadows and streams

SIMILAR SPECIES: Female **Afranius Duskywing** (page 256) cannot be differentiated in the field. **Pacuvius Duskywing** (page 254) has more contrasting gray and brown mottling and longer and more pointed *fw*.

Common Checkered-Skipper ♦ *Pyrgus communis* 261a, b

KEY FIELD MARKS: Indistinguishable from **White Checkered-Skipper** in the field (see Note); *upf* (**261a**) with four rows of white spots, row of small marginal white spots does **not** go to tip; *unh* (**261b**) one **black** spot along **inner costa**.

SIZE: $7/8$–$1^1/4$ inches   ADULTS FLY: late May to early October

HOST PLANTS: **Indian mallow, desert five spot, cheeseweed, checker mallow, alkali mallow, globe mallow, apricot mallow**

RANGE: roughly northern and eastern Arizona (Also: CA, NV, UT, CO, NM)

HABITAT: open areas

NOTE: Can be separated from **White Checkered-Skipper** in the field only where ranges do not overlap; i.e., in northeast would be **White Checkered-Skipper** and in the southwest would be **Common Checkered-Skipper**.

White Checkered-Skipper ♦ *Pyrgus albescens* no photo

KEY FIELD MARKS: Indistinguishable in the field from **Common Checkered-Skipper**; *upf* with four rows of white spots, row of small marginal white spots **does not** go to tip; *unh* one **black** spot near base of leading edge sometimes connected with a faint black line to a lower spot to make what resembles a **telephone receiver**.

SIZE: 1–$1^1/4$ inches   ADULTS FLY: all year weather permitting

HOST PLANTS: same as **Common Checkered-Skipper**

RANGE: roughly throughout Arizona except for the northeast one third (Also: CA, NV, UT, CO, NM)   HABITAT: low desert, foothills, gardens

SIMILAR SPECIES: See **Common Checkered-Skipper**. **Tropical Checkered-Skipper** *ups* base has a mat of gray hairs and *unh* leading edge has **three** dark spots, the middle one rectangular. **Desert Checkered-Skipper** (page 262) *ups* lacks mat of hairs, but like **Tropical** the marginal row of small white dots in the *upf* go all the way to the tip.

Tropical Checkered-Skipper ♦ *Pyrgus oileus* 261c, d

KEY FIELD MARKS: *ups* (**261c**) with **dense gray hairs** at base; *upf* a white spot just **outside** the **innermost rectangular spot** nearest the costa; *unh* (**261d**) **three** dark spots along costa.

SIZE: 1–$1^1/4$ inches   ADULTS FLY: early March to mid June and early September to November

HOST PLANTS: not known in state—elsewhere species in Mallow

RANGE: southeast (Also: NM)   HABITAT: riparian areas

SIMILAR SPECIES: Both **Tropical Checkered-Skipper** and **Desert Checkered-Skipper** (page 262) have *upf* marginal row of white spots that go all the way to the tip. **Desert** lacks mat of gray hairs on *ups* base and *unh* has no dark spots on leading edge but has four spots in a row on cell below leading edge. Also *unh* **Desert** lacks many marks, so appears whiter than **Tropical**.

Desert Checkered-Skipper ♦ *Pyrgus philetas* 263a, b

KEY FIELD MARKS: *unh* (**263b**) no dark spots along the leading edge, but four dark spots in a row the next cell down; rest of *unh* almost all white with very faint markings; *ufw* small white marginal dots go **all the way** to the tip.

SIZE: 1–1$\frac{1}{4}$ inches

ADULTS FLY: all year, weather permitting

HOST PLANTS: species in the mallow family

RANGE: southeast Arizona (Also NM)

HABITAT: desert, washes, fields, gardens

SIMILAR SPECIES: **Common** (page 260) and **White Checkered-Skippers** (page 260) *upf* small white marginal spots do not go to the tip. See **Tropical Checkered-Skipper** (page 260).

Erichson's White-Skipper ♦ *Heliopetes domicella* 263c

KEY FIELD MARKS: *upf* broad white median band; *unh* a wide tan marginal band and tan median band.

SIZE: 1–1$\frac{1}{4}$ inches

ADULTS FLY: all year, weather permitting

HOST PLANTS: **Indian mallow** and *Herissantia*

RANGE: central west to southwest across southern part of Arizona (Also: CA, NV, NM)

HABITAT: desert canyons, near streams

SIMILAR SPECIES: **Laviana White-Skipper** (page 264) has similar *unh* pattern but lacks white *fw* median band.

Northern White-Skipper ♦ *Heliopetes ericetorum* 263d

KEY FIELD MARKS: *upf* apex with dark V's pointing forward; *unh* marginal band's inner edge not straight.

SIZE: 1–1$\frac{1}{2}$ inches

ADULTS FLY: early May to mid-June and mid-September to November (two broods)

HOST PLANTS: **rose mallow, desert five spot, trailing mallow, apricot mallow, globe mallow**

RANGE: throughout except for southern edge of Arizona (Also: CA, NV, UT, CO, NM)

HABITAT: desert washes, chaparral

SIMILAR SPECIES: **Laviana White-Skipper** (page 264) has dark patch at base *unh* and dark patches near *unf* apex.

Common Streaky-Skipper ♦ *Celotes nessus* 265a

KEY FIELD MARKS: *ups* streaks of dark and light radiating to margin

SIZE: $^7/_8$–1 inch

ADULTS FLY: late February to mid-September (two broods)

HOST PLANTS: **Indian mallow, globe mallow**

RANGE: roughly central west through central to the southeast in Arizona (Also: CA, NM)

HABITAT: riparian, open scrub, gardens

Laviana White-Skipper ♦ *Heliopetes laviana* 265b, c

KEY FIELD MARKS: *upf* tan apex with **diagonal white band**; *unh* darker marginal band with **inner edge straight** and a **three-pronged** median band

SIZE: $1^1/_4$–$1^5/_8$ inches

ADULTS FLY: mid-April to early May and mid- September to mid November (two broods or periods of influx)

HOST PLANTS: not known in Arizona—but uses species in Mallow family elsewhere

RANGE: along southern border of Arizona except for extreme southwest

SIMILAR SPECIES: See **Erichson's** (page 262) and **Northern** (page262) **White-Skippers.**

Common Sootywing ♦ *Pholisora catullus* 267a, b

KEY FIELD MARKS: *fw* (**267a**) has a curved postmedian band of **five white spots**; *unh* (**267b**) no spots.

SIZE: $7/8$–1 inch

ADULTS FLY: mid-April to early October (two broods)

HOST PLANTS: several species of **amaranth, Lamb's quarters, Spanish tea, Pitseed goosefoot, red scale**

RANGE: throughout Arizona except extreme southwest and north central to extreme northeast (Also: CA, NV, UT, CO, NM)

HABITAT: many open areas, riparian, gardens

Mojave Sootywing ♦ *Hesperopsis libya* 267c

KEY FIELD MARKS: *unh* large white spots; *ups* fringes **not** checkered; *fw* two faint rows of spots on outer margin.

SIZE: 1–$1^1/4$ inches

ADULTS FLY: April to late July and September through October (two broods)

HOST PLANT: **four wing salt bush**

RANGE: extreme north, west and southern Arizona (Also: CA, NV, UT, NM)

HABITAT: alkali flats, riparian, sagebrush desert

SIMILAR SPECIES: the only Sootywing with large white *unh* spots and uncheckered fringes

Saltbush Sootywing ♦ *Hesperopsis alpheus* 267d

KEY FIELD MARKS: *upf* two pale spots **along outer costa, checkered** fringes.

SIZE: $3/4$–$1^1/8$ inches

ADULTS FLY: early March to late May and early July to early September (two broods)

HOST PLANT: **four wing salt bush**

RANGE: extreme northern, the southeast and a strip across Arizona below the Mogollon Rim from southeast to northwest

HABITAT: saltbush flats

SIMILAR SPECIES: **MacNeill's Sootywing** (page 268), a subspecies of **Saltbush Sootywing**, has more **rounded** *fw* apex and white spots on *ups* that are **not** along the outer costa.

MacNeill's Sootywing ♦ *Hesperopsis alpheus gracielae* 269a

KEY FIELD MARKS: *ups* checkered fringes, **rounded *fw*** apex, pale white spots.

SIZE: $5/8$–1 inch

ADULTS FLY: April to mid-May

HOST PLANT: **Quail-bush**

RANGE: extreme west in the Colorado River Valley and the Bill Willams Delta of Arizona

HABITAT: saltbush flats along rivers

SIMILAR SPECIES: See **Saltbush Sootywing** (page 266)—only possible overlap is in the extreme northwest.

Russet Skipperling ♦ *Piruna pirus* 269b

KEY FIELD MARKS: *unh* **reddish brown** with **no** spots; *unf* three white spots at subapex, other tiny spots below.

SIZE: $7/8$–1 inch

ADULTS FLY: May through June

HOST PLANTS: not known—probably grasses

RANGE: central and central east to extreme north central and extreme northeastern Arizona

HABITAT: mountain meadows and streamsides

Four-spotted Skipperling ♦ *Piruna polingi* 269c,d

KEY FIELD MARKS: *fw* (**269d**) nine scattered white spots on dark brown; *unh* (**269c**) **four spots**.

SIZE: $3/4$–1 inch

ADULTS FLY: June through August

HOST PLANTS: not known—probably grasses

RANGE: roughly central through southeastern Arizona (Also: NM)

HABITAT: mountain meadows and streamsides

Many-spotted Skipperling ◆ *Piruna cingo* 271a, b

KEY FIELD MARKS: *upf* (**271a**) two rows of white spots; *unh* (**271b**) many white oval spots with rectangular spot in center.

SIZE: $3/4$–$7/8$ inch

ADULTS FLY: August through early September

HOST PLANT: **sideoats grama**

RANGE: south-central portion of southeastern Arizona (mostly Santa Cruz County)

HABITAT: grassland and streamside in oak woodland

SIMILAR SPECIES: **Roadside-Skippers** (page 308–321)—but none has **Many-spotted Skipperling**'s distinctive pattern.

Julia's Skipper ◆ *Nastra julia* 271c, d

KEY FIELD MARKS: *uns* (**271c**) orangish-brown (or yellowish-brown) tips; *unh* without light veins; *upf* (**271d**) yellow spots.

SIZE: $7/8$–$1\,1/8$ inches

ADULTS FLY: April through October

HOST PLANT: **Bermuda grass**

RANGE: western border in Colorado River Valley except for the extreme northwest of Arizona (Also: CA, NV)

HABITAT: open grassy areas, gardens

SIMILAR SPECIES: **Eufala Skipper** (page 318) is **gray-brown** with distinctive sub-apical *fw* spots.

Clouded Skipper ◆ *Lerema accius* 273a, b

KEY FIELD MARKS: *uns* (273a) silvery or **bluish-silvery** along trailing edge; *unh* wide median brown area between silvery; *fw* (273b) a large white median spot with two satellite spots and three vertical spots near outer costa.

SIZE: 1³/₈–1³/₄ inches

ADULTS FLY: mid-April to early December

HOST PLANT: **Johnson grass**

RANGE: extreme southeastern Arizona (Also: NM)

HABITAT: woodland edges, riparian

SIMILAR SPECIES: **Umber Skipper** (page 300) has two large yellowish patches on *unh*; spots on *fw* yellowish.

Garita Skipperling ◆ *Oarisma garita* 273c

KEY FIELD MARKS: *unf* orange with narrow black trailing edge border; *unh* with **pale veins, orange inner margin** and white fringe with narrow dark border.

SIZE: ³/₄–1¹/₈ inches

ADULTS FLY: June through August

HOST PLANTS: **squirreltail grass, pine dropseed, needlegrass, bluegrass, blue grama**

RANGE: north-central to northeast and south through mountains to extreme southeastern Arizona

HABITAT: mountain meadows, grasslands and streams

SIMILAR SPECIES: **Edward's Skipperling** (page 274) lacks pale *unh* veins, is always orange above, and has dark fringes.

Orange Skipperling ♦ *Copaeodes aurantiacus* 275a

Key Field Marks: *uns* unmarked orange; *unf* tip not rounded; *unf* and *uph* base with **dark patch**.

SIZE: 1–1$\frac{1}{8}$ inches

ADULTS FLY: all year, weather permitting

HOST PLANTS: **Bermuda grass, blue grama, sideoats grama**

RANGE: throughout Arizona except northeast and central east (Also: CA, NV, UT, CO, NM)

HABITAT: streams, washes, moist canyons, gardens

SIMILAR SPECIES: **Tropical Least Skipper** (page 276) has *fw* apex **rounded** and *uph* with **wide, dark margin** along leading edge.

Edwards' Skipperling ♦ *Oarisma edwardsii* 275b, c

KEY FIELD MARKS: *ups* (**275c**) orange with **dark fringes**; *unh* (**275b**) **dusky** with **brownish-yellow inner margin**.

SIZE: $\frac{7}{8}$–1 inch

ADULTS FLY: late June to mid-August

HOST PLANTS: not known

RANGE: southeast, central east, and along the upper edge of the Mogollon Rim of Arizona (Also: CO, NM)

HABITAT: bunchgrass in pine-oak and juniper woodlands

SIMILAR SPECIES: See **Garita Skipperling** (page 272).

Tropical Least Skipper ♦ *Ancyloxypha arene* 277a, b

KEY FIELD MARKS: *unf* (**277a**) rounded at apex; *uph* (**277b**) wide dark border along costa, narrow dark border at the trailing edge.

SIZE: $7/8$–1 inch

ADULTS FLY: early July to mid-November

HOST PLANTS: **barnyard grass** and **water bentgrass**

RANGE: southeastern Arizona (Also: NM)

HABITAT: moist cienagas, streams

SIMILAR SPECIES: See **Orange Skipperling** (page 274).

Southern Skipperling ♦ *Copaeodes minimus* 277c

KEY FIELD MARKS: *unh* **white** horizontal streak.

SIZE: $1/2$–$3/4$ inch

ADULTS FLY: late August to late September

HOST PLANT: **Bermuda grass**

RANGE: extreme southeastern Arizona (mostly Santa Cruz County)

HABITAT: open areas

SIMILAR SPECIES: **Orange Skipperling** (page 274) does not have *unh* white streak; **Sunrise Skipper** (page 276) has *unh* yellowish streak and black outer veins on *ups*.

Sunrise Skipper ♦ *Adopaeoides prittwitzi* 277d

KEY FIELD MARKS: *unh* **whitish yellow** horizontal streak; *ups* narrow **black** outer border with **black** outer veins, fringes **orange**.

SIZE: $7/8$–1 inch

ADULTS FLY: mid-May to mid-October in two broods

HOST PLANT: **knot grass**

RANGE: extreme southeastern Arizona (Also: NM)

HABITAT: springs

SIMILAR SPECIES: See **Southern Skipperling**.

Fiery Skipper *Hylephila phyleus* 279a, b, c

KEY FIELD MARKS: *unh* (279a) dark spots on yellowish ground; male *ups* (279b) narrow jagged outer borders, stigma separated form nearest outer dark patch; female *ups* (279c) similar to male but outer border and brown patches wider, lacks black stigma.

SIZE: 1$^1/_4$–1$^1/_2$ inches

ADULTS FLY: all year, weather permitting

HOST PLANTS: **Bermuda grass**, **Kentucky bluegrass**

RANGE: throughout Arizona (Also: CA, NV, UT, CO, NM)

HABITAT: open areas, towns

SIMILAR SPECIES: **Woodland Skipper** (page 296) male *upf* **lacks** jagged dark borders and stigma is **connected** to adjacent outer brown patch.

Morrison's Skipper *Stinga morrisoni* 281a, b

KEY FIELD MARKS: *unh* (**281a**) **silvery spike** from base; **male** *upf* (**281b**) narrow stigma, outer adjoining spot separate, rectangular.

SIZE: 1–1$\frac{1}{4}$ inches

ADULTS FLY: late February to late May

HOST PLANTS: not known in Arizona

RANGE: eastern and southeastern Arizona (Also: CO, NM)

HABITAT: oak-juniper and pine-juniper woodlands

Common Branded Skipper *Hesperia comma* 281c

KEY FIELD MARKS: *unh* outer spot band irregular, largest inner spot like a **comma**.

SIZE: 1$\frac{1}{8}$–1$\frac{1}{4}$ inches

ADULTS FLY: early June to late August

HOST PLANTS: **red fescue, blue grama**

RANGE: northwestern Arizona following and above the Mogollon Rim to the White Mountains and Mt. Graham (Also: CA, NV, UT, CO, NM)

HABITAT: mountain meadows and highland grassy areas

SIMILAR SPECIES: See **Juba Skipper**.

Juba Skipper *Hesperia juba* 281d

KEY FIELD MARKS: *uph* slightly translucent so underside shows through; *unh* slightly greenish, lowest spot on outer band indented **inward**; *upf* dark wide **jagged outer border**.

SIZE: 1–1$\frac{1}{2}$ inches

ADULTS FLY: May through mid-June and September (two broods)

HOST PLANTS: **Kentucky bluegrass, slender hairgrass, needlegrass, red brome**

RANGE: roughly across the northern borderlands of Arizona (Also: CA, NV, UT, CO, NM)

HABITAT: grassy openings in sagebrush and pine-juniper woodland

SIMILAR SPECIES: **Common Branded Skipper** bottom outer spot **not** indented inward; **Nevada Skipper** (page 282) bottom outer spot **more indented inward**; both **lack** *upf* jagged outer border of **Juba Skipper**.

Rhesus Skipper ♦ *Polites rhesus* 283a

KEY FIELD MARKS: *unh* **dark** patches contrast with extensive white bands; **white veins**.

SIZE: 1–1$\frac{1}{8}$ inches

ADULTS FLY: May through June

HOST PLANT: **blue grama**

RANGE: from central Arizona along the Mogollon Rim into the White Mountains on the eastern border

HABITAT: highland grasslands

SIMILAR SPECIES: See **Uncas Skipper**.

Uncas Skipper ♦ *Hesperia uncas* 283b

KEY FIELD MARKS: *unh* complex white spot bands, **white** veins.

SIZE: 1$\frac{1}{4}$–1$\frac{5}{8}$ inches

ADULTS FLY: mid-May to late April and mid-August to mid-September (two broods)

HOST PLANT: **blue grama**

RANGE: from the northwest across Arizona north of the Mogollon Rim then down the eastern quarter to the southeast (Also: CA, NV, UT, CO, NM)

HABITAT: undisturbed grassland

SIMILAR SPECIES: **Rhesus Skipper** has **black patches** in *unh*.

Nevada Skipper ♦ *Hesperia nevada* 283c

KEY FIELD MARKS: *unh* lowest white spot in outer spot band strongly indented inward.

SIZE: 1–1$\frac{1}{4}$ inches

ADULTS FLY: June through July

HOST PLANTS: **bottlebrush squirreltail, sheep fescue**

RANGE: White Mountains and extreme north-central Arizona (Also: CA, NV, UT, CO, NM)

HABITAT: high elevation grassland

SIMILAR SPECIES: See **Juba Skipper** (page 280)—overlap in north-central only.

Carus Skipper ♦ *Polites carus* 285a, b

KEY FIELD MARKS: *unh* (285a) grayish-yellow, pale veins, note dark spots on outer veins; *ups* (285b) brownish with white spots.

SIZE: $7/8$–$1^1/8$ inches

ADULTS FLY: mid-March to late May and late June to mid- September (two or three broods)

HOST PLANTS: not known—probably grasses

RANGE: from central Arizona extending in a strip below the Mogollon Rim to the southeast (Also: CA, CO, NM)

HABITAT: grassy areas in oak woodland

Green Skipper ♦ *Hesperia viridis* 285c

KEY FIELD MARKS: *unh* yellow-green with lower outer spots forming a *concave* outer edge.

SIZE: 1–$1^1/4$ inches

ADULTS FLY: late July to mid-August

HOST PLANTS: **blue grama, sideoats grama, slim tridens, buffalo grass**

RANGE: eastern part of Arizona reaching to the northwest in a strip along the Mogollon Rim and spreading along the southeast (Also: CO, NM)

HABITAT: canyons, grasslands

SIMILAR SPECIES: **Pahaska Skipper** outer line of the three lower outer *unh* spots is **convex**, not concave as in **Green Skipper**.

Pahaska Skipper ♦ *Hesperia pahaska* 285d

KEY FIELD MARKS: *unh* orange brown, lower outer spots form a **convex** outer edge.

SIZE: 1–$1^1/2$ inches

ADULTS FLY: mid-February to early June and mid-July to early December (two to three broods)

HOST PLANT: **blue grama**

RANGE: throughout Arizona except for the southwest corner (Also: CA, NV, UT, CO, NM)

HABITAT: desert grassland, foothill grassland

SIMILAR SPECIES: See **Green Skipper**.

Apache Skipper ♦ *Hesperia woodgatei* 287a

KEY FIELD MARKS: *unh* **dark brown** with white **rounded** spots.

SIZE: $1^3/_8$–$1^5/_8$

ADULTS FLY: mid-September through October

HOST PLANTS: not known in area—grasses and sedges elsewhere

RANGE: roughly along the Mogollon Rim to central east and southeastern Arizona (Also: CO, NM)

HABITAT: highland grassland and mountain meadows in pine forests

SIMILAR SPECIES: Other look-alike skippers—**Common Branded** (page 280), **Juba** (page 280), **Green** (page 284)—fly much earlier. Even if there is some overlap when the others fly late, the **Apache Skipper**'s *unh* are **darker** brown and the bands are not as wide and the spots are **rounder**.

Sachem ♦ *Atalopedes campestris* 287b, c, d

KEY FIELD MARKS: **male** *ups* (**287c**) with wide stigma; **female** *ups* (**287d**) with two glassine spots just outside the dark central area; *unh* (**287b**) outer spot band irregular but continuous and lower part of band has darker brown in front of it.

SIZE: $1^3/_8$–$1^5/_8$ inches

ADULTS FLY: early April to early November

HOST PLANTS: **bermuda grass, red fescue, crab grass**

RANGE: throughout Arizona (Also: CA, NV, UT, CO, NM)

HABITAT: many kinds of open areas

Sandhill Skipper ♦ *Polites sabuleti tecumseh* 289a

KEY FIELD MARKS: *unh* spider web appearance, third and fourth (from the top) spots of outer band elongated, **yellowish veins**, curved U-shaped band at bottom; **male *upf* orange above and below stigma.**

SIZE: 3/4–1 inch

ADULTS FLY: April though October

HOST PLANTS: **Bermuda grass, Kentucky bluegrass**

RANGE: western and northern border regions, northern half of eastern border region of Arizona (Also: CA, NV, UT, CO, NM)

HABITAT: mountain meadows, alkali flats

SIMILAR SPECIES: **Males above**—Taxiles Skipper (page 290) **lacks** stigma; **Peck's Skipper** has **narrow** stigma, **all brown** (no orange) below stigma; **Draco Skipper** (page 292) has **large** stigma with **very faint patches of orange** in the brown below the stigma. *unh*—Taxiles Skipper has a **very elongated** middle spot in the outer band; **Peck's Skipper lacks** the yellow veins of the **Sandhill Skipper; Draco Skipper:** the spots in the upper part of outer band **do not touch** the rest of the spots and are not as rectangular as the others.

Lindsey's Skipper ♦ *Hesperia lindseyi* no photo

KEY FIELD MARKS: *unh* yellowish-brown, spots large, yellow to cream, extending along veins; small dark points in the outer margin at the end of each vein.

SIZE: 7/8–1 1/4 inches

ADULTS FLY: May to early June

HOST PLANTS: native grasses (species apparently not known in Arizona)

RANGE: extreme southwestern Arizona in the Colorado River Valley (Also: CA)

HABITAT: open areas with grass

SIMILAR SPECIES: **Common Branded Skipper** (page 280)—no overlap in Arizona

Peck's Skipper ♦ *Polites peckius* 289b, c

KEY FIELD MARKS: *unh* (**289b**) **third spot** in outer band more **elongated**, brown around yellow spots; **male *upf* (289c) brown** below stigma, orange above it.

SIZE: 1–1 1/4 inches

ADULTS FLY: July and August

HOST PLANTS: **Kentucky bluegrass, rice cutgrass**

RANGE: White Mountains on the eastern border of Arizona (Also CO)

HABITAT: mountain meadows and grassland

SIMILAR SPECIES: See **Sandhill Skipper.**

Taxiles Skipper ♦ *Poanes taxiles* 291a, b, c

KEY FIELD MARKS: *unh* (**291a**) middle spot in outer band **very elongated**; in **female** (**291c**) spots are faint in violet-brown; **male** *upf* (**291b**) orange, **lacking stigma**.

SIZE: $1^3/_8$–$1^5/_8$ inches

ADULTS FLY: mid-June to late September

HOST PLANTS: **Kentucky blue grass, Nuttall alkali grass, quackgrass, bluestem, orchard grass, Canada wild rye**

RANGE: northern and central across to eastern and south to southeastern Arizona (Also: UT, CO, NM)

SIMILAR SPECIES: See **Sandhill Skipper** (page 288).

Draco Skipper ♦ *Polites draco* 293a, b

KEY FIELD MARKS: *unh* (**293a**) outer band **white**, veins **not** light, **middle spots elongated**; male *upf* (**293b**) large stigma with **faint patches of orange below stigma.**

SIZE: $7/8$–$1\,1/8$ inches

ADULTS FLY: May through July

HOST PLANTS: not known—probably grasses

RANGE: north central to northeastern Arizona, south to the Mogollon and the White Mountains (Also: NV, UT, CO, NM)

HABITAT: mountain meadows and grasslands

SIMILAR SPECIES: See **Sandhill Skipper** (page 288).

Tawny-edged Skipper ♦ *Polites themistocles* 293c

KEY FIELD MARKS: *uph* usually with no spots; *upf* orange on middle edge; **male** stigma sinuous (in three parts).

SIZE: $7/8$–$1\,3/8$ inches

ADULTS FLY: May through July

HOST PLANTS: **Kentucky bluegrass** and other grasses

RANGE: in the White Mountains of the eastern border extending northwest along the Mogollon Rim of Arizona (Also: UT, CO, NM)

HABITAT: mountain meadows

Sonoran Skipper ♦ *Polites sonora sonora* 295a, b, c

KEY FIELD MARKS: *unh* (**295a**) spots in outer spot band **the same size**, postbasal spot; **male** *upf* (**295b**) wide brown submarginal band with mostly orange around the stigma; **female** *upf* (**295c**) light spots around brown center.

SIZE: $5/8$–$1 1/4$ inches

ADULTS FLY: June through August

HOST PLANTS: not known in Arizona—probably grasses

RANGE: barely enters north-central Arizona (Also: CA, NV, UT, CO)

HABITAT: meadows

NOTE: Race in Arizona has a more greenish-gray *unh*.

Long Dash ♦ *Polites mystic* 297a, b

KEY FIELD MARKS: *unh* (**297a**) broad yellowish outer spot band with the upper two spots **indented and longish**, yellowish postbasal spot; **male** *upf* (**297b**) **yellowish spots** above and below stigma; **female** *upf* black basal patch.

SIZE: $1^{1}/_{8}$–$1^{1}/_{2}$ inches

ADULTS FLY: June through July

HOST PLANTS: **quackgrass, barnyard grass, timothy**

RANGE: central Arizona along middle portion of Mogollon Rim (Also CO)

HABITAT: streams, marshes

SIMILAR SPECIES: **Woodland Skipper** has much smaller indistinct postbasal spot (no overlap in Arizona).

Woodland Skipper ♦ *Ochlodes sylvanoides* 297c, d

KEY FIELD MARKS: *unh* (**297c**) wide outer spot band with upper two spots **strongly indented forward**; **male** *upf* (**297d**) narrow stigma with orange above and below, faint brown area outside and **connected** to the stigma.

SIZE: $^{3}/_{4}$–$1^{1}/_{8}$ inches

ADULTS FLY: July through August

HOST PLANTS: **bermuda grass, wild rye**

RANGE: extreme northwest to north central Arizona (Also: CA, NV, UT, CO, NM)

HABITAT: grasslands near streams, chaparral

SIMILAR SPECIES: See **Long Dash** (no overlap in state).

Delaware Skipper ♦ *Anatrytone logan* 299a, b

KEY FIELD MARKS: *unh* (299a) yellow-orange with **no spots**; **male** *upf* (299b) no stigma, narrow outer margin, outer veins black; black mark at end of cell; **female** *upf* outer veins black, wide black outer margin, black mark at end of cell.

SIZE: 1–1⁵/₈ inches

ADULTS FLY: June

HOST PLANTS: **big bluestem, switchgrass**

RANGE: White Mountains of eastern Arizona (Also: CO, NM)

HABITAT: mountain meadows

Yuma Skipper ♦ *Ochlodes yuma* 299c, d

KEY FIELD MARKS: *unh* (299c) **pale** with **no spots**; *unf* **pale apex** contrasting with light orange; **male** *upf* (299d) orange surrounding narrow stigma, narrow brown border on outer edge.

SIZE: 1–1³/₄ inches

ADULTS FLY: June through September

HOST PLANT: **common reed**

RANGE: extreme north and northwestern Arizona south along Colorado River to and including Bill Williams Delta

HABITAT: marshes in dry areas near host plant

Umber Skipper ♦ *Poanes melane* 301a, b

KEY FIELD MARKS: *unh* (301a) reddish-brown with **two vague yellowish spots**, *upf* (301b) **four yellowish spots** under costal spots.

SIZE: 1-1¼ inches

ADULTS FLY: late April to mid-June (rare)

HOST PLANTS: **tufted hairgrass, Bermuda grass**

RANGE: extreme southeastern Arizona (Also: CA)

HABITAT: streams and canyons in mountains

SIMILAR SPECIES: **Clouded Skipper** (page 272) **lacks** the vague yellowish spots on *unh*, spots on *fw* white.

Snow's Skipper ♦ *Paratrytone snowi* 301c, d

KEY FIELD MARKS: *unh* (301c) **orange-brown** with **vague yellowish** spot band; *unf* (301d) light spots just outside dark base.

SIZE: 1¾–1⅜ inches

ADULTS FLY: early June to late September

HOST PLANT: **pine dropseed**

RANGE: eastern Arizona and along the Mogollon Rim to the north central

HABITAT: mountain and foothill streams and ravines

Dun Skipper ♦ *Euphyes vestris* 303a, b

KEY FIELD MARKS: *uns* usually unmarked brown with **brown fringe**; **male (303a)** often has orange head; **female (303b)** *fw* has small white spots

SIZE: 1–1³/₈ inches

ADULTS FLY: June through July

HOST PLANT: **sedge (***Carex geophila***)**

RANGE: northern to central eastern—excluding southwestern half and extreme southeastern corner of Arizona

HABITAT: highland streams and other moist areas

SIMILAR SPECIES: **Orange-headed** (page 320) and **Orange-edged Roadside-Skippers** (page 318) have orange heads but they have either white or orange fringes.

Deva Skipper ♦ *Atrytonopsis deva* 303c, d

KEY FIELD MARKS: *unh* (**303c**) **brown** with a vague **dark** postmedian line and a **white fringe**; *fw* **lacks** hour glass spot near costa

SIZE: 1¹/₂–1⁵/₈ inches

ADULTS FLY: late April to early July

HOST PLANTS: not known—probably grasses

RANGE: central to southeastern Arizona (Also NM)

HABITAT: grassy areas in oak woodland, streamsides

SIMILAR SPECIES: **Moon-marked Skipper** (page 304) **flies later**, has **dark bluish-brown** *unh* and an **hour glass shaped spot** near mid-costa. **Viereck's Skipper** (page 378) flies at the same time as **Deva**—but it also has an hourglass-shaped spot near mid-costa.

Moon-marked Skipper ♦ *Atrytonopsis lunus* 305a, b

KEY FIELD MARKS: *unh* (**305a**) **dark bluish-brown** with **white or yellowish** fringe; *uph* (**305b**) has **hourglass spot** near mid-costa.

SIZE: 1^1/$_2$–1^3/$_4$ inches

ADULTS FLY: mid-July to late August

HOST PLANT: probably **bullgrass**

RANGE: central to southeastern Arizona (Also NM)

HABITAT: streams in oak woodland

SIMILAR SPECIES: See **Deva Skipper** (page 302).

White-barred Skipper ♦ *Atrytonopsis pittacus* 305c, d

KEY FIELD MARKS: *unh* (**305c**) **white** postmedian bar, uncheckered **white** fringes; **antennae white** below the club; *ups* **305d**.

SIZE: 1^1/$_4$–1^3/$_8$ inches

ADULTS FLY: late February to early June and late August to late October (two broods)

HOST PLANT: not known—probably grasses

RANGE: central to southeastern Arizona (Also NM)

HABITAT: oak woodland, grasslands

SIMILAR SPECIES: See **Python Skipper** (page 306).

Python Skipper ◆ *Atrytonopsis python* 307a

KEY FIELD MARKS: *unh* gray with **narrow and irregularly white spotted** outer band, fringes checkered.

SIZE: 1$\frac{1}{4}$–1$\frac{1}{2}$ inches

ADULTS FLY: late April to mid-July

HOST PLANTS: not known—probably grasses

RANGE: roughly northwest through central to southeastern Arizona (Also: NV, NM)

HABITAT: oak woodland openings and streamsides

SIMILAR SPECIES: **White-barred Skipper** *unh* (page 304): **simple** white outer bar, antennae **white** and fringes **uncheckered. Cestus Skipper** *unh* has prominent **postbasal spot** and **wider** outer spot band.

Cestus Skipper ◆ *Atrytonopsis cestus* 307b

KEY FIELD MARKS: *unh* **brownish**-gray, outer band **jagged** with a prominent **postbasal middle spot.**

SIZE: 1$\frac{1}{8}$–1$\frac{3}{8}$ inches

ADULTS FLY: mid-April to late May and mid-August to early October (two broods)

HOST PLANTS: not known—probably grasses

RANGE: southeastern Arizona

HABITAT: canyons and gullies in thorn scrub grasslands

SIMILAR SPECIES: See **Python Skipper.**

Sheep Skipper ◆ *Atrytonopsis edwardsii* 307c, d

KEY FIELD MARKS: *unh* **mottled gray** with white spots (variable); *uph* has small postbasal spot; *upf* **hourglass spot** near mid costa, **checkered fringes.**

SIZE: 1$\frac{1}{4}$–1$\frac{1}{2}$ inches

ADULTS FLY: early April through June and late July to mid-October (two broods)

HOST PLANTS: **sideoats grama**

RANGE: south central to southeastern Arizona (Also NM)

HABITAT: steep-sided canyons

SIMILAR SPECIES: **Moon-marked Skipper** (page 304) has *unh* bluish-brown and fringes not checkered. **White-barred Skipper** (page 304) has single bar on *unh* and fringes not checkered.

Bronze Roadside-Skipper ◆ *Amblyscirtes aenus* 309a, b

KEY FIELD MARKS: *unh* (**309a**) grayish-brown with many **vague white** postmedian spots (or none); *ups* brown with **orangish tint**; *upf* orangish spots; *unf* (**309b**) whitish postmedian band with **orangish cast** forward of the top half of band; fringes checkered.

SIZE: 1–1 1/4 inches

ADULTS FLY: late April to late September

HOST PLANTS: **sideoats grama**

RANGE: roughly eastern half of Arizona (Also: UT, CO, NM)

HABITAT: streams in brushy and woodland areas

SIMILAR SPECIES: **Bronze Roadside-Skipper** and the others below all have **some orange** in the *unf*. **Oslar's Roadside-Skipper** (page 310): *unh* is gray; fringes **grayish** slightly checkered. **Texas Roadside-Skipper** (page 312): *unh* is gray; yellowish *fw* postmedian spots; **fringe tan** checkered **brown**. **Cassus Roadside-Skipper** (page 310): *unf* **distinctly orange** all the way to the costa. **Large Roadside-Skipper** (page 310): *unh* **dark gray brown** with spots rounder and more distinct. **Simius Roadside-Skipper**: *unh* gray with uncheckered **white** fringes.

Simius Roadside-Skipper ◆ *Amblyscirtes simius* 309c, d

KEY FIELD MARKS: white **uncheckered** fringes; *unh* (**309c**) gray with **pale outer spot band**; *unf* orange inward from postmedian band; *upf* (**309d**) orange in middle with vague orange spot band, **larger orange spot** above that band.

SIZE: 7/8–1 inch

ADULTS FLY: late June to late August

HOST PLANT: **blue grama**

RANGE: central eastern to southeastern and from central eastern below the Mogollon Rim to central part of Arizona (Also: CO, NM)

HABITAT: grasslands

Large Roadside-Skipper ♦ *Amblyscirtes exoteria* 311a

KEY FIELD MARKS: *unh* brown with small round white spots .

SIZE: 1–1¼ inches

ADULTS FLY: mid-June to early September

HOST PLANT: **bullgrass**

RANGE: central to southeastern Arizona (Also NM)

HABITAT: oak woodland and coniferous forest

SIMILAR SPECIES: See **Bronze Roadside-Skipper** (page 308). **Dotted Roadside-Skipper** (page 314) *unh* dark gray with small white spots **narrowly outlined in black**.

Cassus Roadside-Skipper ♦ *Amblyscirtes cassus* 311b, c

KEY FIELD MARKS: fringes checkered; *unh* (**311b**) **mottled gray**; *unf* strongly **orange** in upper middle **including costa**; *upf* (**311c**) orange spots in a sinuous band and an **orange cell spot** above the band.

SIZE: 1 inch

ADULTS FLY: mid-June to early September

HOST PLANT: **bulb panicum**

RANGE: central through eastern Arizona except for the northeast

HABITAT: middle to high elevation woodlands

Oslar's Roadside-Skipper ♦ *Amblyscirtes oslari* 311d

KEY FIELD MARKS: fringes grayish, slightly checkered; *unh* **gray** with faint whitish postmedian band; *upf* **rusty brown** with pale spots (or none).

SIZE: 1⅛–1⅜ inches

ADULTS FLY: early July to early September

HOST PLANTS: not known in Arizona but **sideoats grama** used in other areas

RANGE: roughly central eastern to southeastern and southeastern to south-central Arizona (Also: CO, NM)

HABITAT: canyon bottoms in woodland areas

Texas Roadside-Skipper ♦ *Amblyscirtes texanae* 313a, b

KEY FIELD MARKS: fringes tan checkered brown; *unh* gray with faint postmedian band; *upf* two yellowish postmedian spots and small spot above (sometimes absent); *uph* paler in the middle, darker on the border.

SIZE: 1 inch

ADULTS FLY: mid-July to mid-September

HOST PLANT: bulb panicum

RANGE: southeastern Arizona (Also: NM)

HABITAT: dry washes in low elevation areas

SIMILAR SPECIES: See Bronze Roadside-Skipper (page 308).

Toltec Roadside-Skipper ♦ *Amblyscirtes tolteca prenda* 313c, d

KEY FIELD MARKS: fringes grayish-white with narrow dark checks; *unh* (313c) grayish with clear white postmedian and basal spots, the middle basal spot slightly elongated; *upf* (313d) blackish with many white spots including hourglass shaped spot below mid-costa.

SIZE: 7/8–1 inch

ADULTS FLY: mid-May to mid-September

HOST PLANTS: not known

RANGE: southeastern to south central Arizona

HABITAT: desert grasslands, open woodland, riparian

SIMILAR SPECIES: Dotted Roadside Skipper (page 314) lacks *fw* hourglass spot below mid-costa and has white *unh* dots surrounded narrowly with black.

NOTE: This species was formerly called Prenda Roadside-Skipper *Amblyscirtes prenda*.

Dotted Roadside-Skipper ♦ *Amblyscirtes eos* 315a

KEY FIELD MARKS: *unh* dark gray with **clear white spots narrowly outlined with black**; *ups* solid black with a few postmedian spots.

SIZE: 1 1/4 inches

ADULTS FLY: early March through mid-October (at least two broods)

HOST PLANT: **vine mesquite**

RANGE: northwestern and southeastern Arizona (Also: CO, NM)

HABITAT: canyons in juniper-oak woodland

SIMILAR SPECIES: See **Large Roadside-Skipper** (page 310).

Elissa Roadside-Skipper ♦ *Amblyscirtes elissa* 315b, c

KEY FIELD MARKS: *unh* (**315b**) brown with small white postmedian spot band; *upf* dark (**315c**) brown with postmedian white spot band with **one spot forward** of the band.

SIZE: 7/8–1 inch

ADULTS FLY: mid-July to late August

HOST PLANT: **sideoats grama**

RANGE: only in Santa Cruz County and sothwestern Cochise County in southeastern Arizona (Also: NM)

HABITAT: oak woodland, dry desert washes, riparian

SIMILAR SPECIES: **Large Roadside Skipper** (page 310) found in higher oak and pine habitats than **Elissa**—but both fly together in the Atascosa Mountains, Santa Cruz County (Jim Brock—*pers. comm.*).

Slaty Roadside-Skipper ♦ *Amblyscirtes nereus* 315d

KEY FIELD MARKS: fringes whitish, **very slightly** checked; *unh* **grayish-yellow** with pale whitish spots; *unf* **apex and costal margin** grayish-yellow; *uph* charcoal with **postmedian white spots**.

SIZE: 1 inch

ADULTS FLY: early July to late August

HOST PLANTS: not known—probably grasses

RANGE: southeastern Arizona (Also: NM)

HABITAT: grasslands, streams in oak and mixed woodland

Nysa Roadside-Skipper ♦ *Amblyscirtes nysa* 317a, b

KEY FIELD MARKS: fringes white, checkered brown; *unh* (317a) gray with **blackish patches**; *upf* (317b) **blackish** with white spots.

SIZE: 1–1$\frac{1}{8}$ inches

ADULTS FLY: mid-March to early October (several broods)

HOST PLANTS: **crabgrass** and other grasses

RANGE: southeastern Arizona (Also: NM)

HABITAT: rocky canyons, woodland edges, gardens

Common Roadside-Skipper ♦ *Amblyscirtes vialis* 317c, d

KEY FIELD MARKS: fringes tan, checkered black; *unh* (317c) gray but **nearly black at base** with faint postmedian spots; hind margin and *unf* apex with violet-gray; *upf* (317d) black with four subapical spots.

SIZE: 1–1$\frac{1}{8}$ inches

ADULTS FLY: May through June

HOST PLANTS: not known—probably grasses

RANGE: extreme north-central Arizona (Also: CA, UT, CO, NM)

HABITAT: open areas, streamsides

Orange-edged Roadside-Skipper ♦ *Amblyscirtes fimbriata* 319a

KEY FIELD MARKS: blackish wings with **orange fringe**; head **orange**.

SIZE: 1–1$^1/_4$ inches

ADULTS FLY: late May to late August

HOST PLANTS: **nodding brome, Arizona wheatgrass**

RANGE: southeastern Arizona in Huachuca and Chiricahua Mountains only (Also: NM)

HABITAT: grassy areas in coniferous and juniper-oak woodlands

SIMILAR SPECIES: See **Orange-headed Roadside-Skipper** (page 320).

Eufala Skipper ♦ *Lerodea eufala* 319b

KEY FIELD MARKS: *unh* **gray** to tan, sometimes with small dots; *upf* has semicircle of spots.

SIZE: 1$^1/_8$–1$^3/_8$ inches

ADULTS FLY: late January to mid-December (several broods)

HOST PLANTS: **Bermuda grass, Johnson grass**

RANGE: roughly western Arizona through central and south to the southeast (Also: CA, NV, UT, NM)

HABITAT: open areas, gardens

SIMILAR SPECIES: **Julia's Skipper** (page 270) is **orange to yellow-brown** with **indistinct** sub-apical *fw* spots. **Olive-clouded Skipper** has an *unh* **brown median band**.

NOTE: After landing usually gives one or two wing flaps, i.e., quick slight opening and closing of wings.

Olive-clouded Skipper ♦ *Lerodea dysaules* 319c

KEY FIELD MARKS: *unh* **faint** white postmedian spots behind a **slightly darker brown** median patch.

SIZE: $^7/_8$–1 inch

ADULTS FLY: late February to late June and early August to mid-December (two broods)

HOST PLANTS: observed using **Bermuda grass** and **green spangletop** in Tucson (Bailowitz and Brock 1991)

RANGE: roughly southern Arizona except the very extreme southwest

HABITAT: desert, mesquite forest, gardens

SIMILAR SPECIES: See **Eufala Skipper**.

Orange-headed Roadside-Skipper ♦ *Amblyscirtes phylace* 321a

KEY FIELD MARKS: charcoal wings with **whitish fringe**; **head orange**

SIZE: 1 inch

ADULTS FLY: early July to early August

HOST PLANTS: **big bluestem** and possibly other grasses

RANGE: east central to southeastern Arizona (Also: CO, NM)

HABITAT: ravines in grasslands and open woodland

SIMILAR SPECIES: **Orange-edged Roadside-Skipper** (page 318) has orange fringes; **Dun Skipper** (page 302) lacks colored fringes.

Brazilian Skipper ♦ *Calpodes ethlius* 321b

KEY FIELD MARKS: *unh* three to four **diamond-shaped translucent** spots; *upf* large **squarish** translucent spot with smaller satellite spots

SIZE: 2–2³⁄₈ inches

ADULTS FLY: mid-July to mid-November

HOST PLANT: **common canna**

RANGE: roughly southern Arizona (Also: CA, NM)

HABITAT: gardens with host plant, moist areas as a stray

Orange Giant-Skipper ♦ *Agathymus neumoegeni* no photo

KEY FIELD MARKS: *ups* with extensive orange and broad black margins

SIZE: 2–2³/₈ inches

ADULTS FLY: mid-September to mid-October

HOST PLANT: **Parry's agave**

RANGE: central to central eastern Arizona (Also: NM)

HABITAT: mountains with Parry's agave

SIMILAR SPECIES: **Giant-Skippers** of the genus *Agathymus* are usually found with their wings closed near their host plants making them difficult if not impossible to identify in the field. Best identified by location, time and the host plant. In Arizona the **Orange Giant-Skipper** does not overlap with either the **Arizona** or the **Huachuca Giant-Skipper** (page 324), but does overlap with **Poling's Giant-Skipper** (page 322) in the central part of the state. However, **Poling's Giant-Skipper** is not found in moist watercourses but is found on rocks among its host plants—**Schott's Agave** and **Toumey's Agave**. Poling's Giant-Skipper silhouette seems slightly more convex than other *Agathymus*.

Poling's Giant-Skipper ♦ *Agathymus polingi* 323 a, b

KEY FIELD MARKS: *unh* (**323a**) postmedian band and other spots only faintly prominent; *upf* (**323b**) postmedian band yellow orange

SIZE: 1⁵/₈–1³/₄ inches

ADULTS FLY: late September to early November

HOST PLANTS: **Schott's agave, Toumey's agave, Shindagger**

RANGE: southeastern Arizona

HABITAT: rocky areas near dense stands of host plants—does not go to moisture.

SIMILAR SPECIES: **Orange Giant-Skipper** *ups* brighter orange; **Arizona Giant-Skipper** *unh* post median band fainter, *ups* post median band more orange.

NOTE: Unlike other *Agathymus*, **Poling's Giant-Skipper** is not found along moist water courses, but perches on rocks among its host plants.

Arizona Giant-Skipper *Agathymus aryxna* 323c, d

KEY FIELD MARKS: *unh* (**323c**) very similar to **Huachuca** (page 324) and **Poling's Giant-Skipper**; *upf* (**323d**) orange postmedian band

SIZE: 2–2³/₈ inches

ADULTS FLY: September to mid-November

HOST PLANTS: **Palmers agave, desert agave**

RANGE: southeastern Arizona (Also: NM)

HABITAT: canyons, flats, and grasslands with host plants; attracted to moisture

Huachuca Giant-Skipper ◆ *Agathymus evansi* 325a, b

KEY FIELD MARKS: very similar to **Arizona Giant-Skipper** (page 322)—they overlap only at middle elevations in the Huachuca Mountains. Note in photograph **325b** that wider orange *fw* band touches cell spots (in females).

SIZE: $1^3/_4$–$2^1/_4$ inches

ADULTS FLY: early August to mid-November

HOST PLANT: **"Huachuca" Parry's agave**

RANGE: restricted to the Huachuca Mountains in the southeast of Arizona

HABITAT: oak-juniper and pine-oak woodlands with host plant; attracted to moisture

SIMILAR SPECIES: **Arizona Giant-Skipper** (page 322) has smaller *fw* spots, narrower *fw* postmedian band. Overlaps only in upper limits of **Palmer's Agave** and lower limits of **"Huachuca" Agave** where these plants overlap.

Mojave Giant-Skipper ◆ *Agathymus alliae* no photo

KEY FIELD MARKS: very similar to **Arizona Giant-Skipper**—but never found in same locality.

SIZE: $2^1/_8$–$2^3/_8$ inches

ADULTS FLY: late August to mid-October

HOST PLANT: **Kaibab agave**

RANGE: northwestern Arizona (Also: CA, NV)

HABITAT: canyons in desert and pine woodlands near its host plant

Yucca Giant-Skipper ◆ *Megathymus yuccae* 325c, d

KEY FIELD MARKS: *unh* (**325c**) has a **prominent white spot** below **broad gray** upper band along leading edge and has **silvery** hind margin on **black** base; *uph* (**325d**) **orangish** marginal band.

SIZE: $1^7/_8$–$3^1/_8$ inches

ADULTS FLY: mid-March to early April

HOST PLANTS: many **yucca** species

RANGE: throughout Arizona except the southwest (Also: CA, NV, UT, CO, NM)

HABITAT: desert, foothills and woodlands where host plants occur

SIMILAR SPECIES: **Strecker's Giant-Skipper** (page 326): *unh* not black at base and with **more** white spots. **Ursine Giant-Skipper** (page 326): *unh* has **two connected white patches** just underneath gray portion of leading edge.

Ursine Giant-Skipper ♦ *Megathymus ursus* 327a

KEY FIELD MARKS: *unh* broad silvery upper edge with **two** prominent diverging **white teardrops** below, black veins.

SIZE: $2^1/_2$–$3^1/_4$ inches

ADULTS FLY: early July to late August

HOST PLANTS: many **yucca** species

RANGE: south central to southeastern Arizona (Also NM)

HABITAT: canyon bottoms where large yuccas occur

SIMILAR SPECIES: See **Yucca Giant-Skipper** (page 324).

Strecker's Giant-Skipper ♦ *Megathymus streckeri* 327b, c

KEY FIELD MARKS: *unh* (**327b**) silvery with several white spots; *upf* (**327c**) white-silvery subapical spots; *uph* white marginal band.

SIZE: $2^1/_2$–3 inches

ADULTS FLY: May

HOST PLANTS: **Bailey yucca, narrowleaf yucca**

RANGE: northern to central eastern Arizona (Also: UT, CO, NM)

HABITAT: grasslands and rocky areas with host plants

SIMILAR SPECIES: **Yucca Giant-Skipper** (page 324) has *unh* black at base with only **one** prominent white spot.

Larvae of Selected Species

The larval stage of the butterfly life cycle is devoted to eating, growing and defecating. It has a completely different ecological niche from the adult—which flies, mates, lays eggs and does not eat but rather sips nectar and other nutrients.

From egg to pupa the larva goes through a series of four to five molts, called **instars**, in which the exoskeleton must be shed for growth to continue. Three hormones control these molts. Stretch detectors send a message to the brain, and the first hormone, **eclosion**, circulates in the blood to stimulate the second hormone, **ecdysone**. Ecdysone activates certain genes in the DNA that cause molting. The third, the juvenile hormone, keeps the insect a larva until the last molt. At the point when the juvenile hormone is turned off, adult parts begin to develop inside the last instar.

Black Swallowtail ♦ *Papilio polyxenes* 329a

Note the similarity in color and pattern to the poisonous **Monarch (341d)** and **Queen (343a)**. This Batesian mimicry may give the **Black Swallowtail** protection from predators that, having tried to eat one of these two species, experienced the vomit reaction.

Two-tailed Swallowtail ♦ *Papilio multicaudata* 329b

The development of prominent eyespots on this late-stage larva makes it appear to be snake-like. When disturbed, a forked organ called the **osmeterium** is protruded from just behind the head, giving off a foul odor which may deter ants and other predators.

Anise Swallowtail ♦ *Papilio zelicaon* early stage 329c

This is typical of other Swallowtail first-stage larvae. Compare to the late-stage larva (**329d**). The white patch breaks up the body pattern and may appear to be a bird dropping.

Anise Swallowtail ♦ *Papilio zelicaon* late stage 329d

The similar color and pattern, compared to the larvae of the **Monarch (341d)** and the **Queen (343a)**, suggest that Batesian mimicry is at work. Note the three true legs and orange forked gland (osmeterium).

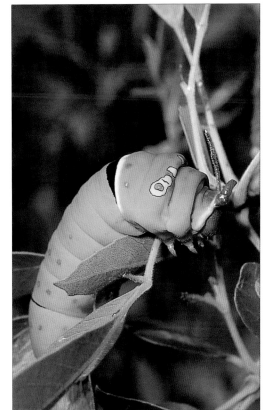

Pipevine Swallowtail ♦ *Battus philenor* eggs and first day larvae 331a

In most species the larva eats the egg shell as part of its first meal. Here the eggs were laid in a cluster under the tip of the host plant leaf.

Pipevine Swallowtail ♦ *Battus philenor* late stage larva, black form 331b

This black larva has protuberances that are a bright orange-red, a warning coloration. Note that the larva is resting on **Wild Cotton** which is not the host plant. It is possible that the small host plant has been devoured and the larva has climbed the cotton bush to rest or to molt.

Pipevine Swallowtail ♦ *Battus philenor* late stage larva, red form 331c

This may be the ultimate in warning coloration. Again note that this larva is not on the host plant.

Spring White ♦ *Pontia sisymbrii* 331d

Note the white dots on the black head and the similarity to the coloration and pattern of the **Monarch** (**341d**) and the **Queen** (**343a**).

Mexican Yellow ♦ *Eurema mexicana* 333a

Note the yellow lateral line and the fainter dorsal yellow line. On *Acacia angustissima*.

Sleepy Orange ♦ *Eurema nicippe* 333b

Very similar to the **Mexican Yellow** except no yellow dorsal line. Both species are very camouflaged on their host plants due to their cryptic coloration and small size.

Cloudless Sulphur ♦ *Phoebis sennae* yellow form 333c

Cloudless Sulphur ♦ *Phoebis sennae* green form 333d

Thicket Hairstreak ♦ *Callophrys spinetorum* 335a

Note the cryptic camouflage. It is interesting that the **Thicket Hairstreak** is very closely related to the **Juniper Hairstreak**. Juniper branches are very similar to this mistletoe, which is the host plant of the **Thicket Hairstreak**. We appreciate the help of Doug Mullins who found the larva.

Gulf Fritillary ♦ *Agraulis vanillae* 335b

Note the warning coloration of red and black. The **passionvine** host plant contains organic cyanide. The black spines may help to ward off parasitoid wasps and **Tachinid** flies.

Variegated Fritillary ♦ *Euptoieta claudia* 335c

Note the similarity to the related **Gulf Fritillary**. These larvae were on *Hybanthus verticillates* in the Violet family.

Theona Checkerspot ♦ *Thessalia theona* 335d

On **Indian paintbrush**

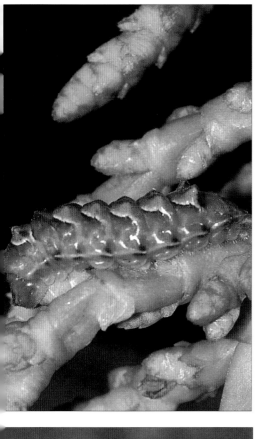

Fulvia Checkerspot ◆ *Thessalia fulvia* 337a

On **Indian Paint-brush** *Castilleja lanata*. Note the differences between this species and the closely related **Theona Checkerspot** (**334d**). **Fulvia** has a prominent black and yellow pattern.

Bordered Patch ◆ *Chlosyne lacinia* 337b

On *Viquiera* sp. (Sunflower family). Eggs are laid in a large cluster on the various host plants. When in the first larval stages, the larvae congregate together, eating the leaves. Later-stage larvae separate. Note the prominent orange spots on the back and the many spines which may protect against ants and parasitoids.

Variable Checkerspot ◆ *Euphydryas chalcedona* 337c

Note the black ground color with tiny white dots and orange protuberances among the numerous black spines.

Tiny Checkerspot ◆ *Dymasia dymas* 337d

Note the white lateral line and short tufts of spines.

American Lady ♦ *Vanessa virginiensis* 339a

The Ladies always spin a web of silk around themselves to protect against parasitoid attacks (see **Painted Lady** 339b). After they have devoured the section of the plant under the silk, however, they have to move to a new spot. The **American Lady** is very distinctive with red-orange spots between rings of yellow and black.

Painted Lady ♦ *Vanessa cardui* 339b

The most widely distributed butterfly in the world, the **Painted Lady** feeds on thistles. Note the large area of the leaf that has been eaten. The spines caught in the silken cover suggest that the larva doesn't eat them.

West Coast Lady ♦ *Vanessa annabella* 339c

This photograph was taken 45 days after the eggs hatched. Because of the great variability in colors of both this species and the **Painted Lady**, they can best be told apart by which plant they are on. The **West Coast Lady** feeds on plants in the Mallow family, the **Painted Lady** on thistles in the Sunflower family.

California Tortoiseshell ♦ *Nymphalis californica* 339d

The host plants are various species of *Ceanothus*. When young, the larvae cluster together. Note the yellow spines.

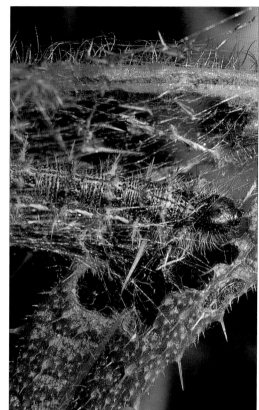

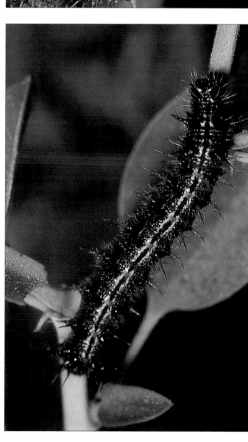

Buckeye ♦ *Junonia sp.* 341a

Note the similarity to the **Variable Checkerspot** (**337c**). The Buckeye has an **orange** head and **black** spines. In identification of any larva, it is important to know the species of the host plant. For instance, this larva was on **Speedwell** (*Veronica sp.*), a host plant for the **Buckeye** but not for the **Variable Checkerspot**.

Red-spotted Admiral ♦ (Red-spotted Purple) *Limenitis arthemis* 341b

The camouflage for the **Red-spotted Admiral** larva is the similarity to a bird dropping. The white represents the uric acid paste found on the outside of bird feces. It is very difficult to tell this larva from the **Viceroy**—also in the genus *Limenitis*—which also feeds on willows (Jim Brock—*pers. comm.*). In this case, the willows were in a location where no **Viceroys** had been seen in recent years but where **Red-spotted Admirals** were present.

Mourning Cloak ♦ *Nymphalis antiopa* 341c

Also found on willows is the distinctive **Mourning Cloak** larva with red-orange triangles on the back and red-orange prolegs (not visible in this photograph). The eggs are laid in a cluster, and the young larvae stay together in the early instars. When a would-be predator approaches, or if the larvae are disturbed, they will jerk their heads up in an aggressive move to protect themselves.

Monarch ♦ *Danaus plexippus* 341d

Moth and butterfly larvae have five pairs of prolegs. The three pairs of true legs on this **Monarch** larva are seen near the top of the photo. With some exceptions, moth caterpillars are generally hairy whereas this larva is smooth-surfaced. Note the similarity to cogeneric **Queen** on the next page. The **Monarch** lacks a third pair of protuberances on the back.

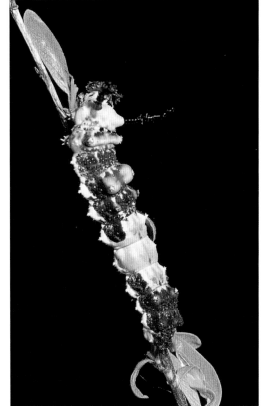

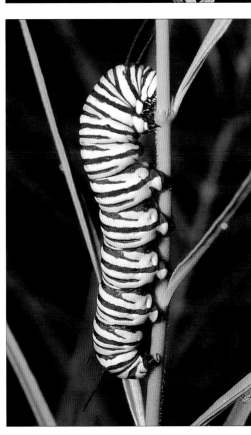

Queen ◆ *Danaus gilippus* 343a

The **Queen** and the **Monarch** are Mullerian mimics in the larval as well as the adult stage. A predator tasting one will learn to leave this pattern alone. The **Queen** is distinguished by having a slightly different white, black and yellow body pattern, by having **three** pairs of long protuberances and by having red at the base of the protuberances.

Northern Cloudywing ◆ *Thorybes pylades* 343b

Identified by Jim Brock while in the field.

Acacia Skipper ◆ *Cogia hippalus* 343c, d

This skipper larva was feeding on *Acacia angustissima* at night. During the day the larva pulls the leaves together with silk and hides in this nest (**343d**). Stewart knows this is the **Acacia Skipper** because he watched the adult lay eggs and followed the larval development. However, the face view is not present, so from these photos one could not be sure that it isn't a **Gold-costa Skipper** (Jim Brock— *pers. comm.*). Once the larva has finished growing, it travels to the ground and pupates in the leaf litter.

Selected Predators and Parasitoids

There are many predators, parasitoids and diseases that attack the egg, larva, pupa and adult. Parasitoids differ from parasites in that the parasitoid *kills* its host. Predators include lizards, frogs, toads, birds, spiders, ladybird, carabid and tiger beetles, assassin and ambush bugs, preying mantids, robber and other flies, dragonflies and wasps. Eight families of wasp are parasitoids on the egg, larva and pupa. They lay their eggs inside the host, which the wasp larva gradually destroys from within.

These animals along with viruses, bacteria and fungi keep populations of butterflies in check. Female butterflies may lay hundreds of eggs, but only two need to survive to keep the population stable.

Jumping Spider with moth caterpillar 345a

Spiders in this group have four eyes facing forward (two larger and two smaller). They can cock their heads upward to focus these eyes on prey or a potential predator. They don't build webs to catch their prey like the orb-weavers but stalk them on the ground or in vegetation. When they jump to avoid a predator or to capture prey, a silk line is always let out to break their fall.

Black and Yellow Garden Spider ◆ *Argiope sp.* 345b

Many orb-weaving spiders, after quickly injecting a venom, digest the insides of adult butterflies that are caught in their sticky webs. Larger butterflies sometimes free themselves with vigorous fluttering motions that often intimidate the spider.

Green Lynx Spider 345c, d

Lynx Spiders have eight eyes in the same plane around the top part of the head and spiny legs. Stewart watched this spider's astonishingly quick attack on this worn butterfly while it was nectaring. In **345d** another **Green Lynx Spider** is draining an **Elada Checkerspot**.

Crab Spider with a male **Southern Dogface** 347a

Female crab spiders wait in flowers for their prey. Their motionless stance and cryptic coloration conceal them well. The first two pairs of legs are held out and open (like the defensive posture of a crab). When nectar-feeding insects come to the flower, the spider's front legs slowly envelop them; then a paralysing venom is quickly injected. Subsequently the spider makes two neat fang incisions, either through the thorax or the abdomen, and begins to digest the insides of her victim. By using a pumping action, she injects her digestive enzymes and extracts the nutrients needed to produce her eggs. Male crab spiders do not kill prey but sip nectar. In this photograph the upper front wing of the Dogface is visible, so the "dog face" pattern can be seen.

Crab Spider with a **Bordered Patch** 347b

Although most crab spiders wait concealed in flowers to ambush their prey, yellow crab spiders on green vegetation attract prey by imitating a bright yellow flower.

Crab Spider with an **Orange Skipperling** 347c

The Orange Skipperling is a very small prey item for the crab spider, which can kill large bumblebees and wasps, as well.

Crab Spider with a **Red-bordered Satyr** 347d

Note the diminutive brush-foot, which is protruding from under the eye of the Satyr. Normally this foot is concealed close to the body.

Praying Mantis ♦ *Stagmomantis limbata* female with a **Pipevine Swallowtail** 349a)

The praying mantis is a very effective predator on both larval and adult stages of butterflies. They apparently are immune to the chemicals that would make a vertebrate such as a bird or a lizard think twice before attacking this poisonous **Pipevine Swallowtail**. Red flowers like the **Cardinal Flower** *Lobelia cardinalis* are very attractive nectar sources for Swallowtails.

Praying Mantis ♦ *Stagmomantis californica/limbata* nymph with a **Sheep Skipper** 349b

Stewart was stalking this butterfly to take a close-up photograph when he was startled by the extremely quick attack of the mantid. Note the front legs effectively holding the butterfly as it eats the head.

Praying Mantis ♦ *Stagmomantis limbata* female with a **Bordered Patch** 349c

P. Brodkin discovered this killing ground. Apparently the mantis was attracted to a favorite puddling place of the **Bordered Patch** and then became a serial killer, leaving the wings as evidence.

Paper Wasp ♦ *Polistes canadensis* 351a

Female paper wasps overwinter in small groups. In spring and summer they build large, hanging paper nests. Their young are fed pieces of insects and spiders. In this photograph, a female has a piece of a moth caterpillar that she will take to the nest.

Sphecid Wasp ♦ possibly *Sphex sp.* 351b

A problem for wasps (and students of butterflies) is that a random search for caterpillars takes much energy and time. Recent research has revealed factors that help some species of wasps to narrow their search. When a caterpillar chews on a leaf, the leaf releases a volatile chemical (a kind of "S.O.S.") that the wasp can smell. The wasp is attracted to the area and then further homes in using the smell of the caterpillar's feces, which she detects by touching them with her antennae.

Sphecid Wasp ♦ *Ammophila sp.* 351c,d

Ammophila wasps, as shown in these photographs, capture a caterpillar, paralyze it and drag it to a hole the wasp has dug. After laying her eggs in the caterpillar, she places it in the hole and covers it. When the wasp larva hatches, it eats the living caterpillar from within. The caterpillar does not die until just before the wasp larva pupates. The wasp eventually emerges from the ground as an adult.

Robber Fly ♦ *Efferia sp.* 353a

Robber Flies attack a wide variety of insects including butterflies, wasps, dragonflies, bees and other flies. They usually attack while their prey is flying. Here a Green-eyed Fly has been captured. Note the long legs with many spines on the larger Robber Fly.

Tachinid Fly ♦ *Adejearia vexatris* 353b

Members of this family of fly have many spiny hairs on the abdomen and are parasitoids on caterpillars. Some species glue their eggs on the surface of their victims. The eggs hatch and bore inside the host, where the fly larvae selectively eat: they leave the vital organs until last, enabling the flies to develop to the pupal stage before the caterpillar dies.

Assassin Bug ♦ *Apiomerus flaviventris* 353c

The Assassin Bug usually waits near flowers and captures its insect prey with prehensile front legs. A long beak is then driven into the victim's body, and the contents are sucked out.

Ambush Bug ♦ *Phymata americana* 353d

Ambush Bugs have stouter bodies than Assassin Bugs. Here the ambush bug has paralyzed and is possibly eating the butterfly on the left. The butterfly on the right was still flapping its wings as Stewart approached. The front legs of Ambush Bugs are equipped with a vice-like appendage (Noel McFarland—*pers. comm.*), and here it is holding onto the leg of the right-hand butterfly so it can't get away.

Rare Butterflies

We have separated these species from the main text for clarity. Our decisions regarding what species to include are based on Bailowitz and Brock (1991) and Opler (1999). Some of these species are considered hypothetical by Bailowitz and Brock, but we have included them because we think it is beneficial to at least know what the possibilities are and what they look like. This section might also help butterflyers identify some of the species they encounter on their trips across the border into Sonora, Mexico.

All of these butterflies except **Viereck's Skipper**, which has been taken in central east Arizona, have been found in the southeastern part of the state. For a detailed account of the actual records, we refer you to the scholarly analysis in Bailowitz and Brock (1991).

White-dotted Cattleheart ♦ *Parides alopius* 355a

KEY FIELD MARKS: *uph* similar to Pipevine Swallowtail but the Cattleheart has **two rows** of spots; the lower row has white and **red** spots.

SIZE: 3–3^1/$_2$ inches

Ruby-spotted Swallowtail ♦ *Papilio anchisiades* 355b

KEY FIELD MARKS: no tail; *unh* postmedian **pink** spots and marginal **yellow** crescents; *uph* postmedian **pink patch.**

SIZE: 2^1/$_4$–4 inches

Three-tailed Swallowtail ♦ *Papilio pilumnus* 355c

KEY FIELD MARKS: *upf* has **one fewer black** stripe than **Two-tailed** (page 18) and **Western Tiger Swallowtail** (page 16); *uph* has **three tails**, the longest lined with yellow.

SIZE: 3^1/$_8$–3^3/$_4$ inches

Polydamus Swallowtail ♦ *Battus polydamus* 355d

KEY FIELD MARKS: **tailless;** *ups* **one row** of submarginal yellow rectangular spots on the *hw* continuing into smaller spots on *fw*, submarginal row of **wavy reddish spots.**

SIZE: 3^1/$_8$–4^1/$_8$ inches

NOTE: In this photograph the yellow spot band is on the *ups*. The rear part of the *hw* has been torn off, but three reddish wavy spots can be seen on the upper *unh*.

Florida White ◆ *Appias drusilla* 357a, b

KEY FIELD MARKS: **male (357a)** is **all white** above; **female** *ups* **(357b)** has **black border** on *fw* and **yellow** on *hw*.

SIZE: $1^3/_4$–$2^1/_2$ inches

Great Southern White ◆ *Ascia monuste* 357c, d

KEY FIELD MARKS: **blue** antennae clubs; *upf* **(357c) black triangles** on outer edge; *unh* **(357d)** pale yellow with yellow basal spot; *unf* black triangles faintly show through.

SIZE: 2–3 inches

Howarth's White ♦ *Ganyra howarthii* no photo

KEY FIELD MARKS: *upf* white with round **black dot** in cell and black dashes between veins on outer edge.

SIZE: 1$^3/_4$–1$^7/_8$ inches

SIMILAR SPECIES: **Great Southern White** (page 356) **lacks** *fw* cell spot.

Sonoran Marble ♦ *Euchloe guaymasensis* 359a

KEY FIELD MARKS: *unh* space between sparse green marbling **dull white**; *upf* **black** at apex, **pale yellow** patch on sub-apex.

SIZE: 1$^1/_4$–1$^1/_2$ inches

SIMILAR SPECIES: **Pearly Marble** (page 32) has **more extensive** green marbling on *unh* and white between marbling is **pearly**.

Tailed Sulphur ♦ *Phoebis neocypris* 359b

KEY FIELD MARKS: *hw* with prominent **tail-like projection**.

SIZE: 2$^3/_8$–2$^3/_4$ inches

Sonoran Hairstreak ♦ *Hypostrymon critola* 359c

KEY FIELD MARKS: *uns* gray with **numerous short dark streaks**; *unh* with postmedian band and two orange spots at bottom rear.

SIZE: $^3/_4$–1 inch

SIMILAR SPECIES: **Gray Hairstreak** (page 58) **lacks** the numerous dark streaks on *uns*.

Marius Hairstreak ♦ *Rekoa marius* 359d

KEY FIELD MARKS: *unf* **orange** costa at base; *unh* upper orange spot at bottom edge has a **small** area of black; postmedian band **white**.

SIZE: $^7/_8$–1$^1/_4$ inches

SIMILAR SPECIES: **Gray Hairstreak** (page 58) has orange in the *unh* postmedian band, **lacks** orange at base of costa.

Red-lined Scrub-Hairstreak ◆ *Strymon bebrycia* 361a

KEY FIELD MARKS: *unh* postmedian band **orange inwardly, white outwardly**; upper orange spot crescent shaped because of large amount of black inside; submarginal **white spots.**

SIZE: 1 1/8 inches

SIMILAR SPECIES: **Gary Hairstreak** (page 58) has more black and less orange in *unh* postmedian band; lacks white submarginal spots in *unh*.

Tailless Scrub-Hairstreak ◆ *Strymon cestri* 361b

KEY FIELD MARKS: *hw* tailless; unh two blackish bands with **a black submarginal spot.**

SIZE: 7/8–1 1/8 inches

Yojoa Scrub-Hairstreak ◆ *Strymon yojoa* 361c

KEY FIELD MARKS: *unh* **submarginal white band.**

SIZE: 7/8–1 1/4 inches

Long-winged Greenstreak ◆ *Cyanophrys longula* 361d

KEY FIELD MARKS: *unh* **green** with a faint postmedian band, **brownish margin,** and a **dark brown extended angle.**

SIZE: 1–1 1/8 inches

Cyna Blue ◆ *Zizula cyna* 363a

KEY FIELD MARKS: small; *uns* with **many black spots** surrounded by white; **zigzag** submarginal line.

SIZE: $5/8$–$7/8$ inch

Crescent Metalmark ◆ *Apodemia phyciodoides* 363b

KEY FIELD MARKS: *upf* has **two small white spots** near outer costa.

SIZE: $7/8$ inch

SIMILAR SPECIES: **Nais Metalmark** (page 108) has **prominent submarginal black spots** in orange on *ups*.

Maria's Metalmark ◆ *Lasaia maria* 363c

KEY FIELD MARKS: *ups* **dull iridescent blue** with many black spots and dashes; **female** (not pictured) *ups* gray replaces blue of male, **whitish median band**.

SIZE: 1–$1\,1/8$ inches

Isabella's Heliconian ◆ *Eueides isabella* 363d

KEY FIELD MARKS: *unh* with **three black bars** and two rows of marginal white spots; *unf* two rows of irregular **yellow** patches.

SIZE: 3–$3\,1/2$ inches

Rosita Patch ♦ *Chlosyne rosita* 365a

KEY FIELD MARKS: *uph* large **orange** median patch; *upf* **two** rows of white dots.

SIZE: 1$^3/_8$–1$^5/_8$ inches

SIMILAR SPECIES: **Bordered Patch** (page 152) has **narrower** *uph* orange band which continues to *hw* angle.

Red-spotted Patch ♦ *Chlosyne marina* 365b

KEY FIELD MARKS: *uph* black with **yellow band**; *unh* yellow median band with **red submarginal spots.**

SIZE: 1$^1/_2$–1$^3/_4$ inches

SIMILAR SPECIES: **Rosita Patch** *uph* patch is **orangish**; *unh* **continuous** red submarginal band **touches** the yellow median band. **Bordered Patch** (see **Rosita Patch**).

Elf ♦ *Microtia elva* 365c

KEY FIELD MARKS: *ups* **black** with **orange** vertical and horizontal bands.

SIZE: 1–1$^3/_4$ inches

Pale-banded Crescent ♦ *Phyciodes tulcis* 365d

KEY FIELD MARKS: *uph* **yellow** postmedian band with two narrow submarginal bands.

SIZE: 1–1$^1/_2$ inches

SIMILAR SPECIES: **Texan Crescent** (page 158) has **red-orange spots** at base *uph* and narrow postmedian band *unh*.

Malachite ♦ *Siproeta stelenes* 367a,b

KEY FIELD MARKS: *uns* (367a) large **green** patches on tan; *ups* (367b) large **green** patches on black.

SIZE: $2^7/_8$–$3^1/_2$ inches

Blackened Bluewing ♦ *Myscelia cyananthe* 367c

KEY FIELD MARKS: *ups* black with **iridescent blue patches** and bands (mostly on *hw*).

SIZE: $2^1/_8$–3 inches

Dingy Purplewing ◆ *Eunica monima* 369a

KEY FIELD MARKS: *unh* gray-brown with **pinkish** near apex; *unf* **dark central patch** with two white patches near costa.

SIZE: 1⁷/₈–2 inches

Black-patched Cracker ◆ *Hamadryas atlantis* No Photo

KEY FIELD MARKS: *ups* **dark bluish**, no reddish cell bar in *upf*; *unf* has **five black lines** in distal cell, in male all **black** in outer portion.

SIZE: 2³/₄–3¹/₂ inches

SIMILAR SPECIES: **Glaucous Cracker lacks** five black lines in *unf* distal cell and male lacks black outer portion *unf*; *upf* apex with more gray; *uph* eyespots have **orange** scales above black crescent.

Glaucous Cracker ◆ *Hamadryas glauconome* 369b

KEY FIELD MARKS: *ups* **grayish** especially **near apex** of *upf*, no reddish cell bar in *upf*; *uph* eyespots have **orange scales above black crescent.**

SIMILAR SPECIES: See **Black-patched Cracker.**

Many-banded Daggerwing ◆ *Marpesia chiron* 369c,d

KEY FIELD MARKS: **long tail**; *ups* (**369c**) **many brown bands** in black; *uns* (**369d**) basal part light in contrast to darker upper half.

SIZE: 2¹/₂–2⁵/₈ inches

'Cream-banded' Dusky Emperor ♦ *Asterocampa idyja argus* 371a, b

KEY FIELD MARKS: *upf* (371a) median **yellow band**; black outer portion with two white subapex spots; *unh* (371b) brown median line, submarginal eyespots with blue centers; *unf* pale median band with blue submarginal spots.

SIZE: 2–2^1/$_4$ inches

Angled Leafwing ♦ *Anaea glycerium* 371c, d

KEY FIELD MARKS: *fw* edge **wavy**; *hw* **tail**; *upf* orange with dark apex; *uph* **all orange**; *unh* brown with **two** darker bands.

SIZE: 2^3/$_8$–3 inches

SIMILAR SPECIES: Other **Leafwings** (page 206) *fw* edge **not wavy**, and they lack two dark bands on *unh*.

Mercurial Skipper ♦ *Proteides mercurius* 373a

KEY FIELD MARKS: head and thorax **yellow-orange** above; *uph* dark with two or three iridescent blue spot bands; *unh* dark base with short projection at angle.

SIZE: 2$^1/_4$–2$^3/_4$ inches

Wind's Silverdrop ♦ *Epargyreus windi* 373b

KEY FIELD MARKS: **orange** top of head and thorax; *unh* large **silver patch**; *uns* **frosted white** on brown outer edges.

SIZE: 1$^{15}/_{16}$–2$^7/_{16}$ inches

SIMILAR SPECIES: **Silver-spotted Skipper** (page 232) lacks orange head and thorax and frosty white in outer *uns*.

Gold-spotted Aguna ♦ *Aguna asander* 373c

KEY FIELD MARKS: top of head and thorax orange; *unh* median band **silvery-white**.

SIZE: 1$^7/_8$–2$^3/_{16}$ inches

Mexican Longtail ♦ *Polythrix mexicanus* 373d

KEY FIELD MARKS: perches with **wings open**; *upf* with **two rows** of glassine spots; **uph** with two dark bands and white fringe.

SIZE: 1$^1/_2$–1$^3/_4$ inches

SIMILAR SPECIES: **Dorantes Longtail** (page 238) perches with **wings closed, lacks** dark bands on *uph*, has **checkered fringe** and inner row of white spots on *fw* more scattered.

Brown Longtail ♦ *Urbanus procne* 375a

KEY FIELD MARKS: *ups* **dark brown**; *upf* two rows of tiny faint spots next to costa, often only one or two spots in the rows (hard to see); *unh* two dark bands.

SIZE: $1^5/_8$–$1^7/_8$ inches

SIMILAR SPECIES: **Dorantes Longtail** (page 238) and **Long-tailed Skipper** (page 238) have **large** spots on *fw*.

Two-barred Flasher ♦ *Astraptes fulgerator* 375b

KEY FIELD MARKS: *ups* top of head, upper thorax and base of wings **iridescent blue**; *upf* two white bands.

SIZE: $1^7/_8$–$2^3/_8$ inches

Sonoran Banded-Skipper ♦ *Autochton pseudocellus* 375c

KEY FIELD MARKS: **white ring** below the antenna club; *upf* postmedian slightly curved golden band, **whitish spots** at subapex along costa; *unh* two darker bands.

SIZE: $1^1/_4$–$1^5/_8$ inches

SIMILAR SPECIES: **Golden Banded-Skipper** (page 240) has a wider *upf* postmedian band, **yellow spots** at subapex and **lacks** the darker *unh* bands.

NOTE: Apparently extirpated north of the Mexican border. The last record is from Ramsey Canyon in the Huachucas in 1936.

Skinner's Cloudywing ♦ *Achalarus albociliatus* 375d

KEY FIELD MARKS: *fw* has a **pale outer margin**, costa edge not folded over; *hw* has white fringe.

SIZE: $1^{11}/_{16}$–$1^{13}/_{16}$ inches

SIMILAR SPECIES: **Coyote Cloudywing** (page 376) has a costal fold.

Coyote Cloudywing ♦ *Achalarus toxeus* 377a

KEY FIELD MARKS: *fw* has a **short costal fold**; *hw* has a white fringe.

SIZE: 1⅝–1⅞ inches

SIMILAR SPECIES: See **Skinner's Cloudywing** (page 374).

Potrillo Skipper ♦ *Cabares potrillo* 377b, c

KEY FIELD MARKS: *upf* (377b) median silvery spot band—the third spot from the costa is **elongated and looks like a tipped over letter L**; *unh* (377c) brown with two darker bands.

SIZE: 1–1½ inches

Fritzgaertner's Flat ♦ *Celaenorrhinus fritzgaertneri* 377d

KEY FIELD MARKS: *upf* a **wide median silvery spot band** with a **pale spot** surrounded with brown within that band and **five spots** on the sub-apex; *uph* mottled brown.

SIZE: 1½–2 inches

NOTE: Sometimes rests during the mid-day hours upside down on the ceilings of caves, under bridges, etc.

Wind's Skipper ♦ *Windia windi* 379a

KEY FIELD MARKS: *fw* three sub-apex translucent spots and five large spots in center; *hw* margin scalloped; *unh* many **gray** spots.

SIZE: 1^1/$_4$–1^1/$_2$ inches

Vireck's Skipper ♦ *Atrytonopsis vierecki* 379b

KEY FIELD MARKS: fringe **brown**; *unh* two narrow dark brown bands; *fw* three small white rectangles near sub-apex, four larger white spots including an **hourglass shaped spot** in *fw* cell.

SIZE: 1^1/$_4$–1^1/$_2$ inches

SIMILAR SPECIES: **Deva Skipper** (page 302) has *hw* **fringe white, lacks** hour-glass spot in *fw* cell.

Mottled Bolla *Bolla clytius* 379c

KEY FIELD MARKS: *ups* mottled brown; *upf* **tiny white spots** at sub-apex near costa.

SIZE: 1–1^1/$_4$ inches

White Spurwing *Antigonus emorsus* 379d

KEY FIELD MARKS: *hw* margin **scalloped**; *ups* **large white area** on both wings; *upf* sub-apex has two sets of silvery spots.

SIZE: 1^1/$_2$ inches

SIMILAR SPECIES: **White-patched Skipper** (page 248) has much smaller white patches on *ups*.

Hermit Skipper ♦ *Grais stigmatica* 381a

KEY FIELD MARKS: palps **orange below**; *fw* with tiny white spots at sub-apex; *ups* dark brown with **two rows of darker blotches**

SIZE: 1³/₄–2¹/₈ inches

NOTE: Sometimes rests upside down under leaves.

Slaty Skipper ♦ *Chiomara mithrax* 381b

KEY FIELD MARKS: *ups* dark brown with **purple gloss** and tan spots

SIZE: 1⁵/₈–1¹/₂ inches

Faceted Skipper ♦ *Synapte syraces* 381c, d

KEY FIELD MARKS: *unh* (**381c**) mottled tan, white and black with a **large black triangle**; *unf* four orange rectangles at sub-apex near costa; *upf* (**381d**) orange with **black patches**; *uph* orange with **wide black border** at base

SIZE: 1–1¹/₄ inches

Violet-banded Skipper ♦ *Nyctelius nyctelius* 383a

KEY FIELD MARKS: **fringes brown**; *unh* two brown bands with **violet** sheen, **black square** near leading edge.

SIZE: 1–1$^1/_2$ inches

Purple-washed Skipper ♦ *Panoquina sylvicola* 383b

KEY FIELD MARKS: *unh* **purple** with whitish postmedian band; *fw* **long** with elongated spot in cell.

SIZE: 1$^1/_8$–1$^1/_2$ inches

Ocala Skipper ♦ *Panoquina ocola* 383c

KEY FIELD MARKS: *unh* generally **unmarked**; *fw* no spot in cell, **long**.

SIZE: 1$^1/_4$–1$^5/_8$ inches

Appendix

List of Arizona butterflies with their host plants in the order in which they appear in the book. Edited by Richard S. Felger and Michael F. Wilson, Drylands Institute, Tucson, Arizona. *Asterisk denotes non-native species.

SWALLOWTAILS

Black Swallowtail, *Papilio polyxenes*
PARSLEY FAMILY, Apiaceae: dill, *Anethum graveolens*; slender celery; *Cyclospermum leptophyllum (=Apium leptophyllum)*; celery, *Apium graveolens*; poison-hemlock, *Conium maculatum*; American wild carrot, *Daucus pusillus*; anise, *Foeniculum vulgare*; water parsnip, *Berula erecta*; parsnip, *Pastinaca sativa*; wate -hemlock, *Cicuta douglasii*; water parsnip, *Sium suave*. RUE OR CITRUS FAMILY: turpentine broom, *Thamnosma montana*.

Baird's Old World Swallowtail, *Papilio machaon bairdii*
DAISY FAMILY, Asteraceae: *Artemisia dracunculoides*. PARSLEY FAMILY: parsnip, *Pastinaca sativa*; cow parsnip, *Heracleum lanatum*.

Indra Swallowtail, *Papilio indra*
PARSLEY FAMILY: variable spring parsley, *Cymopterus purpureus*; *Cymopterus terebinthinus* var. *petraeus (=Pteryxia petraea)*. CITRUS FAMILY: turpentine broom, *Thamnosma montana*.

Anise Swallowtail, *Papilio zelicaon*
PARSLEY FAMILY: celery, *Apium graveolens*; chuchupate, *Ligusticum porteri*; mountain parsley, *Pseudocymopterus montanus*; *Cymopterus terebinthinus* var. *petraeus (=Pteryxia petraea)*; parsnip, *Pastinaca sativa*; yampa, *Perideridia gairdneri*.

Western Tiger Swallowtail, *Papilio rutulus*
ROSE FAMILY, Rosaceae: chokecherry, *Prunus virginiana*; bitter cherry, *Prunus emarginata*. WILLOW FAMILY, Salicaceae: quaking aspen, *Populus tremuloides*; narrowleaf cottonwood, *Populus angustifolia*; arroyo willow, *Salix lasiolepis*; Pacific willow, *Salix lasiandra*; scouler willow, *Salix scouleriana*; coyote willow, *Salix exigua*. BIRCH FAMILY, Betulaceae: thinleaf alder, *Alnus incana* subsp. *tenuifolia*.

Two-tailed Swallowtail, *Papilio multicaudata*
ROSE FAMILY, Roseaceae: bitter cherry, *Prunus emarginata*; chokecherry, *Prunus virginiana*; Arizona rosewood, *Vauquelinia californica*. OLIVE FAMILY, Oleaceae: single-leaf ash, *Fraxinus anomala*; velvet ash, *Fraxinus velutina*. CITRUS FAMILY, Rutaceae: hoptree, *Ptelea trifoliata* subsp. *angustifolia (=Ptelea angustifolia)*. SYCAMORE FAMILY, Platanaceae: Arizona sycamore, *Platanus wrightii*.

Giant Swallowtail, *Papilio cresphontes*
CITRUS FAMILY, Rutaceae: Arizona mock-orange, *Choisya dumosa* (Sycamore Canyon, MFW). Citrus, *Citrus* spp.; hoptree, *Ptelea trifoliata* subsp. *angustifolia*; white sapote, *Casimiroa edulis* (cultivated trees in Tucson, MFW)

Pipevine Swallowtail, *Battus philenor*
PIPEVINE FAMILY, Aristolochiaceae: Indian root, *Aristolochia watsonii*.

WHITES

Chiricahua White, *Neophasia terlootii*
PINE FAMILY, Pinaceae: ponderosa pine, *Pinus ponderosa*; Apache pine, *Pinus engelmannii (=Pinus latifolia)*.

Pine White, *Neophasia menapia* (northern Arizona)
PINE FAMILY, Pinaceae: ponderosa pine, *Pinus ponderosa*; Colorado pinyon pine, *Pinus edulis*; Douglas-fir, *Pseudotsuga menziesii (=Pinus taxifolia)*.

Spring White, *Pontia sisymbrii*
MUSTARD FAMILY, Brassicaceae: rock cress, *Arabis glabra*; *Arabis perennans*; tansy mustard, *Descurainia incana (=Descurainia richardsonii)*; tansy mustard, *Descurainia pinnata*; lacepod or fringepod, *Thysanocarpus curvipes*.

Checkered White, *Pontia protodice*
MUSTARD FAMILY, Brassicaceae: rock cress, *Arabis glabra;* rock cress, *A. drummondii;* black mustard, **Brassica nigra;* mustard, **Brassica rapa (=Brassica campestris);* pepper grass, **Cardaria draba (=Lepidium draba);* pepper grass, *Lepidium fremontii;* shepherd's purse, **Capsella bursa-pastoris;* tansy mustard, *Descurainia pinnata;* tansy mustard, **Descurainia sophia;* radish, **Raphanus sativus;* and other mustards.

Mustard White, *Pieris napi*
MUSTARD FAMILY, Brassicaceae: rock cress, *Arabis glabra;* rock cress, *Arabis drummondii;* winter cress, *Barbarea orthoceras;* black mustard, *Brassica nigra;* bitter cress, *Cardamine cordifolia;* radish, **Raphanus sativus; Draba aurea; Rorippa islandica.*

Cabbage White *Pieris rapae*
MUSTARD FAMILY, Brassicaceae: rock cress, *Arabis glabra;* black mustard, **Brassica nigra;* shepherd's purse, **Capsella bursa-pastoris; Rorippa islandica;* radish, **Raphanus sativus;* cultivated cabbage and other mustard family cultivars. CAPER FAMILY, Capparaceae: Rocky Mountain beeplant, *Cleome serrulata.*

Becker's White *Pontia beckerii*
MUSTARD FAMILY, Brassicaceae: desert plume, *Stanleya pinnata, Stanleya elata;* rock cress, *Arabis lignifera;* black mustard, **Brassica nigra;* pepper grass, *Lepidium perfoliatum;* tansy mustard, **Descurainia sophia; Descurainia richardsonii;* tumble mustard, **Sisymbrium altissimum.*

Pearly Marble *Euchloe hyantis*
MUSTARD FAMILY, Brassicaceae: rock cress, *Arabis glabra;* squaw cabbage, *Caulanthus crassicaulis;* tansy mustard, *Descurainia pinnata, D. richardsonii;* pepper grass, *Lepidium fremontii,* desert plume, *Stanleya pinnata; Streptanthella longirostris; *Sisymbrium altissimum.*

Large Marble *Euchloe ausonides*
MUSTARD FAMILY, Brassicaceae: cress, *Arabis glabra, Arabis drummondi, Arabis hirsuta, Arabis fendleri;* winter cress, *Barbarea orthoceras;* black mustard, **Brassica nigra;* California tansy mustard, *Descurainia californica,* Richardson tansy mustard, *Descurainia richardsonii,* radish, **Raphanus sativus;* tumble mustard, **Sisymbrium altissimum; Thelypodium lasiophyllum.*

Sara Orangetip *Anthocharis sara*
MUSTARD FAMILY, Brassicaceae: rock cress, *Arabis glabra;* common rock cress, *Arabis perennans; Athysanus pusillus;* winter cress, *Barbarea orthoceras;* *black mustard, *Brassica nigra;* shepherd's purse, **Capsella bursa-pastoris;* tansy mustard, *Descurainia pinnata;* radish, **Raphanus sativus.*

'Pima' Desert Orangetip *Anthocharis cethura pima*
MUSTARD FAMILY, Brassicaceae: tansy mustard, *Descurainia pinnata; Caulanthus lasiophyllus (=Thelypodium lasiophyllum); Streptanthella longirostris.*

SULPHURS

Orange Sulphur *Colias eurytheme*
PEA FAMILY, Fabaceae: loco weed, *Astragalus crassicarpus; Astragalus crotalariae;* wild licorice, *Glycyrrhiza lepidota;* Spanish clover, *Lotus purshianus;* lupine, *Lupinus succulentus;* lupine, *Lupinus bicolor;* bean, *Phaseolus* sp.; Colorado river hemp, *Sesbania herbacea (=Sesbania macrocarpa);* white clover, **Trifolium repens;* red clover, **Trifolium pratense;* Rydberg clover, *Trifolium longipes;* American vetch, *Vicia americana;* medick, *Medicago* sp.

Southern Dogface *Colias cesonia*
PEA FAMILY, Fabaceae: bastard indigo, *Amorpha fruticosa;* stinking willow or mock locust, *Amorpha californica;* alfalfa, **Medicago sativa; Dalea pogonathera; Marina calycosa (=Dalea calycosa); Dalea albiflora; Dalea versicolor* var. *sessilis; (=Dalea wislizeni* var. *sessilis); Marina parryi (=Dalea parryi).*

Clouded Sulphur *Colias philodice*
PEA FAMILY, Fabaceae: ground plum, *Astragalus crassicarpus* var. *cavus;* alfalfa, **Medigo sativa;* burclover; **Medicago polymorpha (=Medicago hispida);* white sweetclover,

386

Melilotus albus; white clover, **Trifolium repens;* red clover, **Trifolium pratense;* Rydberg clover, *Trifolium longipes;* American vetch, *Vicia americana;* sweet vetch, *Hedysarum boreale.*

Queen Alexandra's Sulphur *Colias alexandra*
PEA FAMILY, Fabaceae: loco weed, *Astragalus lentiginosus; Astragalus eremiticus;* sweet vetch, *Hedysarum boreale;* alfalfa, **Medicago sativa;* purple loco, *Oxytropis lambertii;* golden pea, *Thermopsis rhombifolia (=Thermopsis pinetorum);* red clover, **Trifolium pratense;* American vetch, *Vicia americana.*

Lyside Sulphur *Kricogonia lyside*
Host plant not known in Arizona.

White-angled Sulphur *Anteos chlorinde*
Host plant not known in Arizona.

Yellow-angled Sulphur *Anteos maerula*
Host plant not known in Arizona.

Cloudless Sulphur *Phoebis sennae*
PEA FAMILY, Fabaceae: *Senna hirsuta* var. *glaberrima (=Cassia leptocarpa* var. *glaberrima,* the only variety native to Arizona); *Senna covesii (=Cassia covesii); Chamaecrista nictitans* var. *mensalis (=Cassia leptadenia); Senna lindheimeriana (=Cassia lindheimeriana); Senna bauhinioides (=Cassia bauhinoides); Senna wislizeni (=Cassia wislizeni).*

Large Orange Sulphur *Phoebis agarithe*
PEA FAMILY, Fabaceae: feather bush, *Lysiloma watsonii (=Lysiloma thornberi).*

Orange-barred Sulphur *Phoebis philea*
PEA FAMILY, Fabaceae: *Senna hirsuta* var. *glaberrima (=Cassia leptocarpa* var. *glaberrima,* the only variety native to Arizona).*

Boisduval's Yellow *Eurema boisduvaliana*
PEA FAMILY, Fabaceae: *Senna hirsuta* var. *glaberrima (=Cassia leptocarpa* var. *glaberrima,* the only variety native to Arizona).*

Mexican Yellow *Eurema mexicana*
PEA FAMILY, Fabaceae: New Mexican locust, *Robinia neomexicana;* white ball acacia, *Acacia angustissima.*

Tailed Orange *Eurema proterpia*
PEA FAMILY, Fabaceae: *Chamaecrista nictitans* var. *mensalis (=Cassia leptadenia).*

Little Yellow *Eurema lisa*
Host plant not known in Arizona.

Mimosa Yellow *Eurema nise*
Host plant not known in Arizona   uses whitethorn acacia, *Acacia constricta,* in Sonora.

Dina Yellow *Eurema dina*
Host plant not known in Arizona.

Barred Yellow *Eurema daira*
Host plant not known in Arizona

Dainty Sulphur *Nathalis iole*
DAISY FAMILY, Asteraceae: false dogfennel, *Dyssodia papposa;* common beggar tick, *Bidens pilosa;* common sneezeweed, *Helenium autumnale;* cosmos, *Cosmos* sp.; Spanish needles, *Palafoxia arida (=Palafoxia linearis,* sensu lato); Hopi tea, greenthread, *Thelesperma megapotamicum.*

Sleepy Orange *Eurema nicippe*
PEA FAMILY, Fabaceae: *Senna hirsuta* var. *glaberrima (=Cassia leptocarpa* var. *glaberrima,* the only variety native to Arizona); *Senna covesii (=Cassia covesii); Senna lindheimeriana (=Cassia lindheimeriana); Senna wislizeni (=Cassia wislizeni).*

HAIRSTREAKS

Gray Hairstreak *Strymon melinus*
PEA FAMILY, Fabaceae: false indigo, *Amorpha* sp.; locoweed, *Astragalus crotalariae;* wild licorice, *Glycyrrhiza lepidota;* silvery lupine, *Lupinus argenteus;* alfalfa, **Medicago sativa;* white sweetclover, **Melilotus albus;* white clover, **Trifolium repens;* vetch, *Vicia* sp.

MALLOW FAMILY, Malvaceae: cheeseweed, little mallow, *Malva parviflora;* common mallow, *Malva neglecta;* alkali mallow, *Malvella leprosa (=Sida leprosa* var. *hederacea, Sida hederacea);* apricot mallow, *Sphaeralcea ambigua.* BUCKTHORN FAMILY, Rhamnaceae: California buckthorn, *Rhamnus californica.* BUCKWHEAT FAMILY, Polygonaceae: winged buckwheat, *Eriogonum alatum;* willow smartweed, *Polygonum lapathifolium.* STICKLEAF FAMILY, Loasaceae: stickleaf, *Mentzelia* sp. SNAPDRAGON FAMILY, Scrophulariaceae: wooly mullein, *Verbascum thapsus.* MINT FAMILY, Lamiaceae: desert lavender, *Hyptis emoryi;* dead nettle, *Lamium amplexicaule.* SPURGE FAMILY, Euphorbiaceae: *Croton monanthogynus.* MILKWEED FAMILY, Asclepiadaceae: butterfly weed, *Asclepias tuberosa.* BIGNONIA FAMILY, Bignoniaceae: trumpet bush, *Tecoma stans.* BEAR GRASS FAMILY, Nolinaceae: sacahuista, bear grass, *Nolina microcarpa.*

Soapberry Hairstreak *Phaeostrymon alcestis*
SOAPBERRY FAMILY, Sapindaceae: western soapberry, *Sapindus drummondii (= Sapindus saponaria* var. *drummondii).*

Leda Ministreak *Ministrymon leda*
PEA FAMILY, Fabaceae: velvet mesquite, *Prosopis velutina.*

Arizona Hairstreak *Erora quaderna*
BUCKTHORN FAMILY, Rhamnaceae: Fendler ceanothus, *Ceanothus fendleri.* OAK FAMILY, Fagaceae: Arizona white oak, *Quercus arizonica.*

Colorado Hairstreak *Hypaurotis crysalus*
OAK FAMILY, Fagaceae: Gambel oak, *Quercus gambelii.*

Silver-banded Hairstreak *Chlorostrymon simaethis*
Host plant unknown in Arizona.

Xami Hairstreak *Callophrys xami*
STONECROP FAMILY, Crassulaceae: *Graptopetalum bartramii (=Echeveria bartramii); Graptopetalum rusbyi (=Echeveria rusbyi).*

Desert Elfin *Callophrys fotis*
ROSE FAMILY, Rosaceae: quinine bush, *Purshia mexicana (=Cowania mexicana).*

Western Pine Elfin *Callophrys eryphon*
PINE FAMILY, Pinaceae: ponderosa pine, *Pinus ponderosa;* limber pine, *Pinus flexilis.*

Golden Hairstreak *Habroidais grunus*
OAK FAMILY, Fagaceae: oaks, *Quercus* spp.

Brown Elfin *Callophrys augustinus*
HEATHER FAMILY, Ericaceae: manzanita, *Arctostaphylos* sp.; deer brush *Ceanothus integerrimus.*

Ilavia Hairstreak *Satyrium ilavia*
OAK FAMILY, Fagaceae: Sonoran scrub oak, *Quercus turbinella.*

Behr's Hairstreak *Satyrium behrii*
ROSE FAMILY, Rosaceae: bitter brush, *Purshia tridentata.*

Mallow Scrub-Hairstreak *Strymon istapa*
MALLOW FAMILY, Malvaceae: alkali mallow, *Malvella leprosa (=Sida leprosa* var. *hederacea, Sida hederacea)*

Coral Hairstreak *Satyrium titus*
ROSE FAMILY, Rosaceae: common chokecherry, *Prunus virginianus.*

Hedgerow Hairstreak *Satyrium saepium*
BUCKTHORN FAMILY, Rhamnaceae: Fendler ceanothus, *Ceanothus fendleri; Ceanothus greggii.*

Sylvan Hairstreak *Satyrium sylvinus*
WILLOW FAMILY, Salicaceae: sandbar willow, *Salix exigua;* arroyo willow, *Salix lasiolepis.*

'Siva' Juniper Hairstreak *Callophrys gryneus siva*
CYPRESS FAMILY, Curpressaceae: common juniper, *Juniperus communis;* alligator juniper, *Juniperus deppeana.*

'Canyon' Bramble Hairstreak *Callophrys dumetorum apama*
BUCKWHEAT FAMILY, Polygonaceae: buckwheat, *Eriogonum* sp.

'Desert' Sheridan's Hairstreak *Callophrys sheridanii comstocki*
BUCKWHEAT FAMILY, Polygonaceae: buckwheat, *Eriogonum heermanni*.

Great Purple Hairstreak *Atlides halesus*
MISTLETOE FAMILY, Viscaceae: mistletoe, *Phoradendron flavescens* and other *Phoradendron* spp.

Thicket Hairstreak *Callophrys spinetorum*
MISTLETOE FAMILY, Viscaceae: pine mistletoe, *Arceuthobium vaginatum, A. campylodium.*

Creamy Stripe-streak *Arawacus jada*
Host plant unknown in Arizona.

BLUES

Western Pygmy-Blue *Brephidium exile*
GOOSEFOOT FAMILY, Chenopodiaceae: saltbush species: four-wing saltbush, *Atriplex canescens;* bractscale, *Atriplex serena;* spear oracle, *Atriplex patula;* Australian saltbush, **Atriplex semibaccata;* red scale, *Atriplex rosea;* desert holly, *Atriplex hymenelytra;* seepweed, *Suaeda moquinii (=Suaeda torreyana);* goosefoot, *Chenopodium album, Chenopodium leptophyllum;* Russian thistle, **Salsola tragus (=Salsola kali* of authors). CARPET-WEED FAMILY, Aizoaceae: sea purslane, *Sesuvium verrucosum;* horse purslane, *Trianthema portulacastrum.*

Spring Azure *Celastrina ladon*
ROSE FAMILY, Rosaceae: fern-bush, *Chamaebatiaria millefolium;* rock spiraea, *Holodiscus dumosus;* ninebark, *Physocarpus monogynus;* rock-mat, *Petrophytum caespitosum;* chokecherry, *Prunus virginiana.* BUCKTHORN FAMILY, Rhamnaceae: deerbrush, *Ceanothus integerrimus.* DOGWOOD FAMILY, Cornaceae: red osier dogwood, *Cornus stolonifera.* PEA FAMILY, Fabaceae: yellow sweetclover, **Melilotus officinalis;* rattle-box *Crotolaria sagittalis;* cliff bush, *Jamesia americana* (Saxifrage Family)

Ceraunus Blue *Hemiargus ceraunus*
PEA FAMILY, Fabaceae: whiteball acacia, *Acacia angustissima;* locoweed, *Astragalus crotalariae;* alfalfa, **Medicago sativa;* honey mesquite, *Prosopis glandulifera* var. *torreyana (=Prosopis juliflora* var. *torreyana);* screwbean, *Prosopis pubescens.*

Marine Blue *Leptotes marina*
PEA FAMILY, Fabaceae: mesquite, *Prosopis* sp.; stinking willow or mock locust, *Amorpha californica;* catclaw acacia, *Acacia greggii;* wild licorice, *Glycyrrhiza lepidota;* alfalfa, **Medicago sativa;* feather bush, *Lysiloma watsonii (=Lysiloma thornberi).*

Reakirt's Blue *Hemiargus isola*
PEA FAMILY, Fabaceae: whitethorn acacia, *Acacia constricta,* whiteball acacia, *Acacia angustissima;* indigo-bush, *Psorothamnus scoparius (=Dalea scoparia); D. pogonathera;* wild licorice, *Glycyrrhiza lepidota;* alfalfa, **Medicago sativa;* yellow sweetclover, **Melilotus officinalis;* white sweetclover, **Melilotus albus;* sourclover, **Melilotus indica;* Mesquite, *Prosopis juliflora;* white clover, **Trifolium repens;* Rydberg clover, *Trifolium longipes.*

Eastern Tailed-Blue *Everes comyntas*
PEA FAMILY, Fabaceae: Spanish clover, *Lotus purshianus;* lupine, *Lupinis bicolor;* sour clover, **Melilotus indicus;* yellow sweetclover, **Melilotus officinalis;* Alsike clover, **Trifolium hybridum;* white clover, **Trifolium repens;* red clover, **Trifolium pratense;* common vetch, **Vicia sativa;* American vetch, *Vicia americana.*

Western Tailed-Blue *Everes amyntula*
PEA FAMILY, Fabaceae: purple loco, *Oxytropis lambertii;* American vetch, *Vicia americana.*

Dotted Blue *Euphilotes enoptes*
BUCKWHEAT FAMILY, Polygonaceae: Wright's buckwheat, *Eriogonum wrightii.*

Square-spotted Blue *Euphilotes battoides centralis*
BUCKWHEAT FAMILY, Polygonaceae: flat-top buckwheat, *Eriogonum fasciculatum.*

Rita Blue *Euphilotes rita*
BUCKWHEAT FAMILY, Polygonaceae: Wright's buckwheat, *Eriogonum wrightii;* wild buckwheat, *Eriogonum corymbosum;* sorrel buckwheat, *Eriogonum polycladon.*

Spalding's Blue *Euphilotes spaldingi*
> BUCKWHEAT FAMILY, Polygonaceae: red-root buckwheat, *Eriogonum racemosum*.

Melissa Blue *Lycaeides melissa*
> PEA FAMILY, Fabaceae: wild licorice, *Glycyrrhiza lepidota;* sweet vetch, *Hedysarum boreale;* Spanish clover, *Lotus purshianus;* silvery lupine, *Lupinus argenteus;* silky lupine, *Lupinus sericeus (=Lupinus barbiger);* alfalfa, *Medicago sativa.

Acmon Blue *Plebejus acmon*
> BUCKWHEAT FAMILY, Polygonaceae: red-root buckwheat, *Eriogonum racemosum; Eriogonum umbellatum;* Wright's buckwheat, *Eriogonum wrightii;* flat-top buckwheat, *Eriogonum plumatella;* knotweed, **Polygonum aviculare*. PEA FAMILY, Fabaceae: Spanish clover, *Lotus purshianus;* colchita, *Lotus humistratus; Lotus oblongifolus;* freckled milkvetch, *Astragalus lentiginosus;* white sweetclover, *Melilotus alba.

Silvery Blue *Glaucopsyche lygdamus*
> PEA FAMILY, Fabaceae: sweet-vetch, *Hedysarum boreale;* Spanish clover, *Lotus purshianus;* silvery lupine, *Lupinus argenteus;* lupine, *Lupinus succulentus;* silky lupine, *Lupinus sericeus;* purple loco, *Oxytropis lambertii;* common vetch, **Vicia sativa;* American vetch, *Vicia americana*.

Small Blue *Philotiella speciosa*
> BUCKWHEAT FAMILY, Polygonaceae: kidney-leaved buckwheat, *Eriogonum reniforme; Oxytheca perfoliata*.

Arrowhead Blue *Glaucopshyche piasus*
> PEA FAMILY, Fabaceae: lupine, *Lupinus argenteus*.

Arctic Blue *Agriades glandon*
> PRIMROSE FAMILY, Primulaceae: rock jasmine, *Androsace septen triopina;* shooting star, *Dodecatheon alpinum*.

Greenish Blue *Plebejus saepiolus*
> PEA FAMILY, Fabaceae: alsike clover, *Trifolium hybridum;* white clover, **Trifolium repens; Trifolium rusbyi; Trifolium variegatum*.

Boisduval's Blue *Plebejus icarioides*
> PEA FAMILY, Fabaceae: lupine, *Lupinus argenteus; Lupiunus latifolius; Lupinus sitgreausii; Lupinus succulentus; Lupinus palmeri; Lupinus sericeus*.

COPPERS

Ruddy Copper *Lycaena rubidus*
> BUCKWHEAT FAMILY, Polygonaceae: western dock, *Rumex occidentalis;* wild rhubarb, *Rumex hymenosepalus*.

Purplish Copper *Lycaena helloides*
> BUCKWHEAT FAMILY, Polygonaceae: knotweed, *Polygonum ariculare; Polygonum lapathifolium; Polygonum persicaria; Polygonum amphibium; Polygonum douglasii;* curly dock, *Rumex crispus;* wild rhubarb, *Rumex hymenosepalus;* sheep's sorrel, *Rumex acetosella.

Blue Copper *Lycaena heteronea*
> BUCKWHEAT FAMILY, Polygonaceae: flat-top buckwheat-brush, *Eriogonum fasciculatum;* wild buckwheat, *Eriogonum aureum*.

Tailed Copper *Lycaena arota*
> SAXIFRAGE FAMILY, Saxifragaceae: golden currant, *Ribes aureum;* trumpet gooseberry, *Ribes leptanthum;* wax currant, *Ribes cereum*.

METALMARKS

Mormon Metalmark *Apodemia mormo mejicana*
> BUCKWHEAT FAMILY, Polygonaceae: Wright's buckwheat, *Eriogonum wrightii;* corymb buckwheat, *Eriogonum corymbosum;* Mojave buckwheat, *Eriogonum fasciculatum;* desert trumpet, *Eriogonum inflatum;* skeleton weed, *Eriogonum deflexum; Eriogonum leptocladon;* sulfur buckwheat, *Eriogonum umbellatum;* James buckwheat, *Eriogonum jamesi*.

Palmer's Metalmark *Apodemia palmeri*
> PEA FAMILY, Fabaceae: mesquite, *Prosopis* sp.

Nais Metalmark *Apodemia nais*
BUCKTHORN FAMILY, Polygonaceae: Fendler buckbrush, *Ceanothus fendleri.*

Hepburn's Metalmark *Apodemia hepburni*
Host plant unknown in Arizona.

Fatal Metalmark *Calephelis nemesis*
DAISY FAMILY, Asteraceae: seep willow, *Baccharis salicifolia (=Baccharis glutinosa).*

Arizona Metalmark *Calephelis arizonensis*
DAISY FAMILY, Asteraceae: beggar tick, *Bidens* sp.; boneset, *Eupatorium greggii,* suspected.

Ares Metalmark *Emesis ares*
OAK FAMILY, Fagaceae: Mexican blue oak, *Quercus oblongifolia.*

Wright's Metalmark *Calephelis wrighti*
DAISY FAMILY, Asteraceae: sweetbush, *Bebbia juncea.*

Zela Metalmark *Emesis zela*
Host plant not known in Arizona.

BRUSH-FOOTED BUTTERFLIES

American Snout *Libytheana carinenta*
ELM FAMILY, Ulmaceae: desert hackberry, *Celtis pallida;* netleaf hackberry, *Celtis reticulata.*

Gulf Fritillary *Agraulis vanillae*
PASSION FLOWER FAMILY, Passifloraceae: hairy passion flower, *Passiflora foetida; Passiflora* sp.

Zebra Heliconian *Heliconius charithonia*
PASSION FLOWER FAMILY, Passifloraceae: passion flower, *Passiflora* sp., suspected in Arizona.

Variegated Fritillary *Euptoieta claudia*
VIOLET FAMILY, Violaceae: green violet, *Hybanthus verticillatus.* FOUR O'CLOCK FAMILY, Nyctaginaceae: spiderling, *Boerhavia erecta.* MILKWEED FAMILY, Asclepiadaceae: *Metastelma arizonica.* PASSION FLOWER FAMILY, Passifloraceae: hairy passion flower, *Passiflora foetida;*

Mexican Fritillary *Euptoieta hegesia*
PASSION FLOWER FAMILY, Passifloraceae: hairy passion flower, *Passiflora foetida; Passiflora bryoniodes* (suspected).

Nokomis Fritillary *Speyeria nokomis*
VIOLET FAMILY, Violaceae: meadow violet, *Viola nephrophylla.*

Mormon Fritillary *Spcycria mormonia*
VIOLET FAMILY, Violaceae: violets: *Viola nuttallii, Viola nephrophylla, Viola adunca.*

Coronis Fritillary *Speyeria coronis*
VIOLET FAMILY, Violaceae: Nuttall's violet, *Viola nuttallii.*

Atlantis Fritillary *Speyeria atlantis*
VIOLET FAMILY, Violaceae: meadow violet, *Viola nephrophylla;* Nuttall's violet, *Viola nuttallii; Viola purpurea.*

Aphrodite Fritillary *Speyeria aphrodite*
VIOLET FAMILY, Violaceae: Nuttall's violet, *Viola nuttallii;* meadow violet, *Viola nephrophylla.*

Arachne Checkerspot *Polydryas arachne*
FIGWORT FAMILY, Scrophulariaceae: penstemon, *Penstemon cobaea; Penstemon dasyphyllus; Penstemon virgatus;* bearded penstemon, *Penstemon barbatus.*

Sagebrush Checkerspot *Chlosyne acastus*
DAISY FAMILY, Asteraceae: hoary aster, *Aster canescens;* yellow rabbitbrush, *Chrysothamnus viscidiflorus; Machaerantha asteroides.*

Variable Checkerspot *Euphydryas chalcedona*
FIGWORT FAMILY, Scrophulariaceae: Indian paintbrush: *Castilleja lanata, Castilleja integra, Castilleja linariaefolia, Castilleja chromosa;* monkeyflower, *Mimulus nasutus;* bush penstemon, *Keckiella antirrinoides;* penstemon: *Penstemon bridgesii, Penstemon barbatus, Penstemon whippleanus, Penstemon strictus, Penstemon virgatus;* beeplant, *Scrophularia*

californica; lousewort, *Pedicularis centranthera;* water speedwell, *Veronica anagallis-aquatica;* common mullein, **Verbascum thapsus;* hedge nettle, *Stachys palustris.* BROOM-RAPE FAMILY, Orobanchaceae: broom-rape, *Orobanche fasciculata.* PLANTAIN FAMILY, Plantaginaceae: plantain: *Plantago lanceolata, Plantago major.*

Theona Checkerspot *Thessalia theona*
FIGWORT FAMILY, Scrophulariaceae: Indian paintbrush, *Castilleja lanata; Brachystigma wrightii.*

Black Checkerspot *Thessalia cyneas*
FIGWORT FAMILY, Scrophulariaceae: Indian paintbrush, *Castilleja laxa.*

Fulvia Checkerspot *Thessalia fulvia*
FIGWORT FAMILY, Scrophulariaceae: Indian paintbrush, *Castillija lanata, C. integra.*

Leanira Checkerspot *Thessalia leanira*
FIGWORT FAMILY, Scrophulariaceae: Indian paintbrush, *Castilleja lanata*

California Patch *Chlosyne californica*
DAISY FAMILY, Asteraceae: common sunflower, *Helianthus annuus;* golden-eye, *Viguiera deltoidea* sensu lato.

Bordered Patch *Closyne lacinia*
DAISY FAMILY, Asteraceae: ragweed, *Ambrosia artemisiifolia,* blanket flower, *Gaillardia pulchella;* sunflower, *Helianthus annuus, Helianthus ciliaris;* golden-eye, *Viguiera dentata; Viguiera deltoidea,* sensu lato; crown beard, *Verbesina encelioides.*

Silvery Checkerspot *Chlosyne nycteis*
DAISY FAMILY, Asteraceae: coneflower, *Rudbeckia laciniata.*

Tiny Checkerspot *Dymasia dymas*
ACANTHUS FAMILY, Acanthaceae: hummingbird bush, *Justicia californica (=Beloperone californica); Tetramerium hispidum.*

Elada Checkerspot *Texola elada*
ACANTHUS FAMILY, Acanthaceae: desert honeysuckle, *Anisicanthus thurberi.*

Texan Crescent *Phyciodes texana*
ACANTHUS FAMILY, Acanthaceae: *Dicliptera resupinata.*

Tawny Crescent *Phyciodes batesii*
DAISY FAMILY, Asteraceae: *Aster* sp.

Vesta Crescent *Phyciodes vesta*
ACANTHUS FAMILY, Acanthaceae: *Dyschoriste decumbens.*

Phaon Crescent *Phyciodes phaon*
VERBENA FAMILY, Verbenaceae: common frog fruit, *Phyla nodiflora (=Lippia nodiflora);* northern frog fruit, *Phyla lanceolata (=Lippia lanceolata).*

Pearl Crescent *Phyciodes tharos*
DAISY FAMILY, Asteraceae: *Symphyotrichum subulatum (=Aster exilis),* suspected.

Painted Crescent *Phyciodes picta*
MORNING-GLORY FAMILY, Convolvulaceae: field bindweed, **Convolvulus arvensis.* DAISY FAMILY, Asteraceae: *Symphyotrichum subulatum (=Aster exilis),* suspected.

Northern Crescent *Phyciodes selenis*
DAISY FAMILY, Asteraceae: *Aster* sp.

Field Crescent *Phyciodes campestris*
DAISY FAMILY, Asteraceae: Siskiyou aster, *Aster hesperius; Aster foliaceus.*

Pale Crescent *Phyciodes pallida*
DAISY FAMILY, Asteraceae: thistle, *Cirsium* sp.

Mylitta Crescent *Phyciodes mylitta*
DAISY FAMILY, Asteraceae: bull thistle, Canada thistle, **Circium arvense;* milk thistle, **Silybum marianum.* FIGWORT FAMILY, Scrophulariaceae: seep-spring monkeyflower, *Mimulus guttatus.*

Question Mark *Polygonia interrogationis*
ELM FAMILY, Ulmaceae: netleaf hackberry, *Celtis reticulata.*

Satyr Comma *Polygonia satyrus*
NETTLE FAMILY, Urticaceae: tall white nettle, *Urtica gracilis*. WILLOW FAMILY, Salicaceae: willow, *Salix* sp.

Green Comma *Polygonia faunus*
WILLOW FAMILY, Salicaceae: quaking aspen, *Populus tremuloides*.

Hoary Comma *Polygonia gracilis*
SAXIFRAGE FAMILY, Saxifragaceae: wax currant, *Ribes cereum;* white stem gooseberry, *Ribes inerme;* gooseberry currant, *Ribes montigenum*.

California Tortoiseshell *Nymphalis californica*
BUCKTHORN FAMILY, Rhamnaceae: deerbrush, *Ceanothus integerrimus;* buckbrush, *Ceanothus fendleri*.

Milbert's Tortoiseshell *Nymphalis milberti*
NETTLE FAMILY, Urticaceae: tall white nettle, *Urtica gracilis*.

American Lady *Vanessa virginiensis*
DAISY FAMILY, Asteraceae: cud-weed, *Gnaphalium palustre; Gnaphalium purpureum;* Canada thistle, **Cirsium arvense;* milk thistle, **Silybum marianum*. NETTLE FAMILY, Urticaceae: nettle, *Urtica* sp.

Painted Lady *Vanessa cardui*
DAISY FAMILY, Asteraceae: Canada thistle, *Cirsium arvense;* bull thistle, *Cirsium vulgare;* wavyleaf thistle, *Cirsium undulatum;* desert thistle, *Cirsium neomexicanum;* artichoke, **Cynara scolymus;* milk thistle, **Silybum marianum;* musk thistle, **Carduus nutans;* burdock, **Arctium minus;* blessed thistle, **Cnicus benedictus;* estafiata, *Artemisia frigida;* mugwort, *Artemisia ludoviciana;* yellow star-thistle, **Centaurea solstitialis;* pearly everlasting, *Anaphalis margaritacea;* common sunflower, *Helianthus annuus*. BORAGE FAMILY, Boraginaceae: narrow-leaf cryptantha, *Cryptantha angustifolia*. MALLOW FAMILY, Malvaceae: cheese-weed, **Malva parviflora;* common malva, **Malva neglecta;* alkali mallow, *Malvella leprosa (=Sida leprosa* var. *hederacea, Sida hederacea);* apricot mallow, *Sphaeralcea ambigua*. GOOSEFOOT FAMILY, Chenopodiaceae: *Chenopodium album*. PEA FAMILY, Fabaceae: silvery lupine, *Lupinus argenteus;* lupine, *Lupinus succulentus;* alfalfa, **Medicago sativa*. NETTLE FAMILY, Urticaceae: *Urtica* sp. PLANTAIN FAMILY, Platanaceae: English plantain, *Plantago lanceolata*. MUSTARD FAMILY, Brassicaceae: radish, **Raphanus sativus*.

West Coast Lady *Vanessa annabella*
MALLOW FAMILY, Malvaceae: cheeseweed, **Malva parviflora;* common malva, **Malva neglecta;* alkali mallow, *Malvella leprosa (=Sida leprosa* var. *hederacea, Sida hederacea);* trailing mallow, *Fremalche exilis (Malvastrum exile);* apricot mallow, *Sphaeralcea ambigua*.

Red Admiral *Vanessa atalanta*
NETTLE FAMILY, Urticaceae: nettle, *Urtica gracilis;* pellitory, *Parietaria floridana*.

Mourning Cloak *Nymphalis antiopa*
WILLOW FAMILY, Salicaceae: sandbar willow, *Salix exigua;* peach-leaf willow, *Salix amygdaloides;* bebb willow, *Salix bebbiana; Salix lasiandra; Salix gooddingii (=Salix nigra,* misapplied); yellow willow, *Salix lutea;* quaking aspen, *Populus tremuloides*.

Common Buckeye *Junonia coenia*
PLANTAIN FAMILY, Platanaceae: English plantain, *Plantago lanceolata; Plantago virginica; Plantago major*. FIGWORT FAMILY, Scrophulariaceae: toad flax, *Linaria vulgaris;* owl's-clover, *Castilleja exserta (=Orthocarpus purpurascens);* violet twining snapdragon, *Maurandya antirrhiniflora;* speedwell, *Veronica anagallis-aquatica; Veronica americana*. VERBENA FAMILY, Verbenaceae: common frog fruit, *Phyla nodiflora (=Lippia nodiflora);* northern frog fruit, *Phyla lanceolata (=Lippia lanceolata)*. ACANTHUS FAMILY, Acanthaceae: *Ruellia nudiflora*.

Tropical Buckeye *Junonia genoveva (form nigrosuffusa)*
FIGWORT FAMILY, Scrophulariaceae: monkeyflower, *Mimulus* sp.; speedwell veronica, *Veronica anagallis-aquatica*.

Red-spotted Admiral *Limenitus arthemis*
   WILLOW FAMILY, Salicaceae: willow, *Salix* sp.; Fremont cottonwood, *Populus fremontii;* quaking aspen, *Populus tremuloides.* ROSE FAMILY, Rosaceae: chokecherry, *Prunus virginiana.*

Viceroy *Limenitis archippus*
   WILLOW FAMILY, Salicaceae: willow, *Salix exigua;* Fremont cottonwood, *Populus fremontii;* quaking aspen, *Populus tremuloides.*

Weidemeyer's Admiral *Limenitis weidemeyerii*
   WILLOW FAMILY, Salicaceae: sandbar willow, *Salix exigua;* quaking aspen, *Populus tremuloides.* ROSE FAMILY, Rosaceae: chokecherry, *Prunus virginiana;* service berry, *Amelanchier utahensis;* rock spiraea, *Holodiscus dumosus.*

California Sister *Adelpha bredowii*
   OAK FAMILY, Fagaceae: Gambel oak, *Quercus gambelii;* Sonoran scrub oak, *Quercus turbinella;* Arizona white oak, *Quercus arizonica;* Emory oak, *Quercus emoryi.*

Common Mestra *Mestra amymone*
   SPURGE FAMILY, Euphorbiaceae: nose-burn, *Tragia nepetaefolia* (suspected); *Tragia laciniata* (suspected).

Ruddy Daggerwing *Marpesia petreus*
   MULBERRY FAMILY, Moraceae: common fig, **Ficus carica.*

Tropical Leafwing *Anaea aidea*
   SPURGE FAMILY, Euphorbiaceae: *Croton* sp.

Goatweed Leafwing *Anaea andria*
   SPURGE FAMILY, Euphorbiaceae: Texas croton, *Croton texensis.*

Hackberry Emperor *Asterocampa celtis*
   ELM FAMILY, Ulmaceae: netleaf hackberry, *Celtis reticulata.*

Empress Leilia *Asterocampa leilia*
   ELM FAMILY, Ulmaceae: desert hackberry, *Celtis pallida.*

Tawny Emperor *Asterocampa clyton*
   ELM FAMILY, Ulmaceae: netleaf hackberry, *Celtis reticulata.*

Nabokov's Satyr *Cyllopsis pyracmon (check spell for Nabokov)*
   GRASS FAMILY, Poaceae: bullgrass, *Muhlenbergia emersleyi.*

Canyonland Satyr *Cyllopsis pertepida*
   Host plant not known—probably a grass.

Small Wood-Nymph *Cercyonis oetus*
   Host plant not known—probably a grass.

Pine Satyr *Paramacera allyni*
   Host plant not known—probably a grass.

Red Satyr *Megisto rubricata*
   Host plant not known—probably a grass.

Great Basin Wood-Nymph *Cercyonis sthenele*
   GRASS FAMILY, Poaceae: grasses.

Common Wood-Nymph *Cercyonis pegala*
   GRASS FAMILY, Poaceae: wild oats, **Avena fatua; Andropogon* sp. (or related genera).

Mead's Wood-Nymph *Cercyonis meadii*
   GRASS FAMILY, Poaceae: grasses.

Red-bordered Satyr *Gyrocheilus patrobas*
   GRASS FAMILY, Poaceae: bullgrass, *Muhlenbergia emersleyi.*

Common Ringlet *Coenonympha tullia*
   GRASS FAMILY, Poaceae: needle grass, *Stipa* sp.; Kentucky bluegrass, **Poa pratensis.*

Alberta Arctic *Oeneis alberta daura*
   GRASS FAMILY, Poaceae: fescue, *Festuca* sp.

Ridings' Arctic *Neominois ridingsii*
   GRASS FAMILY, Poaceae: blue grama, *Bouteloua gracilis.*

Monarch *Danaus plexippus*
MILKWEED FAMILY, Asclepiadaceae: showy milkweed, *Asclepias speciosa;* butterfly weed, *Asclepias tuberosa;* poison milkweed, *Asclepias subverticillata;* desert milkweed, *Asclepias erosa;* narrow-leaf milkweed, *Asclepias fascicularis;* reed-stem milkweed, *Asclepias subulata.*

Queen *Danaus gilippus*
MILKWEED FAMILY, Asclepiadaceae: white-stem milkweed, *Asclepias albicans;* desert milkweed, *Asclepias erosa;* narrow-leaf milkweed, *Asclepias fascicularis (=Asclepias mexicana* of authors*);* reed-stem milkweed, *Asclepias subulata;* butterfly weed, *Asclepias tuberosa;* vining milkweed, *Sarcostemma cynanchoides.*

Soldier *Danaus eresimus*
Probably milkweeds.

SKIPPERS

Dull Firetip *Pyrrhopyge araxes*
OAK FAMILY, Fagaceae: Arizona white oak, *Quercus arizonica.*

Silver-spotted Skipper *Epargyreus clarus*
PEA FAMILY, Fabaceae: New Mexican locust, *Robinia neomexicana;* bastard indigo, *Amorpha fruticosa;* wild licorice, *Glycyrrhiza lepidota.*

Hammock Skipper *Polygonus leo*
Host plant not known in Arizona.

White-striped Longtail *Chioides catillus*
Host plant not known in Arizona.

Zilpa Longtail *Chioides zilpa*
Host plant not known in Arizona.

Short-tailed Skipper *Zestusa dorus*
OAK FAMILY, Fagaceae: Emory oak, *Quercus emoryi;* Arizona white oak, *Quercus arizonica;* Gambel oak, *Quercus gambelii.*

Arizona Skipper *Codatractus arizonensis*
PEA FAMILY, Fabaceae: kidney wood, *Eysenhardtia orthocarpa.*

Desert Cloudywing *Achalarus casica*
PEA FAMILY, Fabaceae: tick clover, *Desmodium cinerascens;* tick clover, *Desmodium batocaulon;* butterfly pea, *Clitoria mariana.*

Long-tailed Skipper *Urbanus proteus*
PEA FAMILY, Fabaceae: tick clover, *Desmodium neomexicanum;* tick clover, *Desmodium batocaulon;* butterfly pea, *Clitoria mariana;* mesquite, *Prosopis* sp.

Dorantes Longtail *Urbanus dorantes*
PEA FAMILY, Fabaceae: tick clover, *Desmodium neomexicanum;* tick clover, *Desmodium batocaulon.*

Golden Banded-Skipper *Autochton cellus*
PEA FAMILY, Fabaceae: New Mexican locust, *Robinia neomexicana;* butterfly pea, *Clitoria mariana;* desert bean, *Phaseolus filiformis (=Phaseolus wrightii).*

Northern Cloudywing *Thorybes pylades*
PEA FAMILY, Fabaceae: *Cologania angustifolia;* tick clover, *Desmodium batocaulon;* stinking willow or mock locust, *Amorpha californica;* alfalfa, **Medicago sativa;* rosary bean, *Rhynchosia texana;* red clover, **Trifolium pratense;* white clover, **Trifolium repens;* American vetch, *Vicia americana.*

Mexican Cloudywing *Thorybes mexicanus*
PEA FAMILY, Fabaceae: American vetch, *Vicia americana;* Rydberg clover, *Trifolium longipes;* mountain pea, *Lathyrus lanszwertii (=Lathyrus arizonicus)*

Drusius Cloudywing *Thorybes drusius*
PEA FAMILY, Fabaceae: *Cologania angustifolia.*

Acacia Skipper *Cogia hippalus*
PEA FAMILY, Fabaceae: whiteball acacia, *Acacia angustissima.*

Gold-costa Skipper *Cogia caicus*
PEA FAMILY, Fabaceae: whiteball acacia, *Acacia angustissima.*

Golden-headed Scallopwing *Staphylus ceos*
GOOSEFOOT FAMILY, Chenopodiaceae: Fremont's goosefoot, *Chenopodium fremontii.*

Texas Powdered-Skipper *Systasea pulverulenta*
MALLOW FAMILY, Malvaceae: Indian mallow, *Abutilon incanum; Abutilon mollicomum (=Abutilon sonorae);* globe mallow, *Sphaeralcea angustifolia.*

Arizona Powdered-Skipper *Systasea zampa*
MALLOW FAMILY, Malvaceae: Indian mallow, *Abutilon malacum;* Indian mallow, *Abutilon incanum;* Parish mallow, *Abutilon parishii; Abutilon abutiloides; Abutilon reventum;* bladder mallow, *Herissantia crispa.*

White-patched Skipper *Chiomara asychis georgina*
Host plant unknown—MALPHIGIA FAMILY suspected.

Brown-banded Skipper *Timochares ruptifasciatus*
Host plant unknown in Arizona.

Valeriana Skipper *Codatractus mysie*
PEA FAMILY, Fabaceae: *Tephrosia leiocarpa.*

Dreamy Duskywing *Erynnis icelus*
WILLOW FAMILY, Salicaceae: quaking aspen, *Populus tremuloides.*

Sleepy Duskywing *Erynnis brizo burgessi*
OAK FAMILY, Fagaceae: Gambel's oak, *Quercus gambelii;* wavyleaf oak, *Quercus xundulata;* Sonoran scrub oak, *Quercus turbinella.*

Juvenal's Duskywing *Erynnis juvenalis clitus*
OAK FAMILY, Fagaceae: Arizona white oak, *Quercus arizonica;* Emory oak, *Quercus emoryi;* gray oak, *Quercus grisea.*

Rocky Mountain Duskywing *Erynnis telemachus*
OAK FAMILY, Fagaceae: Gambel's oak, *Quercus gambelii.*

Meridian Duskywing *Erynnis meridianus*
OAK FAMILY, Fagaceae: Arizona white oak, *Quercus arizonica.*

Scudder's Duskywing *Erynnis scudderi*
Host plant not known, probably oaks.

Horace's Duskywing *Erynnis horatius*
OAK FAMILY, Fagaceae: Gambel's oak, *Quercus gambelii.*

Mournful Duskywing *Erynnis tristis*
Hostplant not known in Arizona, oaks elsewhere.

Pacuvius Duskywing *Erynnis pacuvius*
BUCKTHORN FAMILY, Rhamnaceae: buckbrush, deer briar, Fendler ceanothus, *Ceanothus fendleri.*

Funereal Duskywing *Erynnis funeralis*
PEA FAMILY, Fabaceae: New Mexican locust, *Robinia neomexicana;* butterfly-pea, *Clitoria mariana;* alfalfa, **Medicago sativa; Coursetia caribaea (=Cracca edwardsii); Galactia wrightii.*

Afranius Duskywing *Erynnis afranius*
PEA FAMILY, Fabaceae: silvery lupine, *Lupinus argenteus;* Spanish clover, *Lotus purshianus.*

Persius Duskywing *Erynnis persius*
PEA FAMILY, Fabaceae: golden pea, *Thermopsis rhombifolia (=Thermopsis pinetorum);* silvery lupine, *Lupinus argenteus;* broad-leaved lupine, *Lupinus latifolius.* WILLOW FAMILY, Salicaceae: quaking aspen, *Populus tremuloides.*

Mountain Checkered-Skipper *Pyrgus xanthus*
ROSE FAMILY, Rosaceae: cinquefoil, *Potentilla pulcherrima.*

Small Checkered-Skipper *Pyrgus scriptura*
MALLOW FAMILY, Malvaceae: alkali mallow, *Malvella leprosa (=Sida hederacea);* globe mallow, *Sphaeralcea coccinea;* apricot mallow, *Sphaeralcea ambigua.*

Common Checkered-Skipper *Pyrgus communis*
 MALLOW FAMILY, Malvaceae: Indian mallow, *Abutilon theophrasti;* desert fivespot,
 Eremalche rotundifolia (=Malvastrum rotundifolium), **Malva neglecta;* cheeseweed, **Malva
 parviflora;* checker mallow, *Sidalcea neomexicana;* alkali mallow, *Malvella leprosa (=Sida
 leprosa* var. *hederacea, Sida hederacea);* globe mallow, *Sphaeralcea angustifolia;* apricot
 mallow, *Sphaeralcea ambigua.*

White Checkered-Skipper *Pyrgus albescens*
 MALLOW FAMILY, Malvaceae: Many of the same mallows as the Common Checkered-
 Skipper.

Tropical Checkered-Skipper *Pyrgus oileus*
 Host plant unknown in Arizona.

Desert Checkered-Skipper *Pyrgus philetas*
 MALLOW FAMILY, Malvaceae: *Sida procumbens* and probably other mallow species.

Erichson's White-Skipper *Heliopetes domicella*
 MALLOW FAMILY, Malvaceae: Indian mallow, *Abutilon incanum;* bladder mallow,
 Herissantia crispa.

Northern White-Skipper *Heliopetes ericetorum*
 MALLOW FAMILY, Malvaceae: rock hibiscus, *Hibiscus denudatus;* desert fivespot, *Eremalche
 rotundifolia (=Malvastrum rotundifolium);* trailing mallow, *Eremalche exilis (Malvastrum
 exile);* apricot globe mallow, *Sphaeralcea ambigua;* globe mallow, *Sphaeralcea angustifolia.*

Common Streaky-Skipper *Celotes nessus*
 MALLOW FAMILY, Malvaceae: Indian mallow, *Abutilon incanum;* globe mallow,
 Sphaeralcea angustifolia.

Laviana White-Skipper *Heliopetes laviana*
 Host plant not known in Arizona—MALLOW FAMILY, Malvaceae, elsewhere.

Common Sootywing *Pholisora catullus*
 AMARANTH FAMILY, Amaranthaceae: Amaranth, *Amaranthus retroflexus, Amaranthus
 hybridus, Amaranthus albus (=Amaranthus graecizans,* of authors). GOOSEFOOT FAMILY,
 Chenopodiaceae: lamb's quarters, *Chenopodium album;* Spanish tea, *Chenopodium
 ambrosioides;* pitseed goosefoot, *Chenopodium berlandieri;* red scale, *Atriplex rosea.*

Mojave Sootywing *Hesperopsis libya*
 GOOSEFOOT FAMILY, Chenopodiaceae: four-wing saltbush, *Atriplex canescens.*

Saltbush Sootywing *Hesperopsis alpheus*
 GOOSEFOOT FAMILY, Chenopodiaceae: four-wing saltbush, *Atriplex canescens.*

MacNeill's Sootywing *Hesperopsis alpheus gracielae*
 GOOSEFOOT FAMILY, Chenopodiaceae: quail bush, *Atriplex lentiformis.*

Russet Skipperling *Piruna pirus*
 Host plant unknown—probably grasses.

Four-spotted Skipperling *Piruna polingi*
 Host plant unknown—probably grasses.

Many-spotted Skipperling *Piruna cingo*
 GRASS FAMILY, Poaceae: sideoats grama, *Bouteloua curtipendula*

Julia's Skipper *Nastra julia*
 GRASS FAMILY, Poaceae: Bermuda grass, **Cynodon dactylon.*

Clouded Skipper *Lerema accius*
 GRASS FAMILY, Poaceae: Johnson grass, **Sorghum halepense*

Garita Skipperling *Oarisma garita*
 GRASS FAMILY, Poaceae: bottlebrush squirreltail, *Elymus elymoides (=Sitanion hystrix);* pine
 dropseed, *Blepharoneuron tricholepis;* Columbia needlegrass, *Stipa columbiana;* Kentucky
 bluegrass, *Poa pratensis;* blue grama, *Bouteloua gracilis.*

Orange Skipperling *Copaeodes aurantiacus*
 GRASS FAMILY, Poaceae: Bermuda grass, **Cynodon dactylon;* sideoats grama, *Bouteloua
 curtipendula.*

Edward's Skipperling *Oarisma edwardsii*
   Host plant not known in Arizona.

Tropical Least Skipper *Ancyloxypha arene*
   GRASS FAMILY, Poaceae: barnyard grass, *Echinochloa crusgalli;* water bentgrass,
   Polypogon viridis (=Agrostis semiverticillata).

Southern Skipperling *Copaeodes minimus*
   GRASS FAMILY, Poaceae: Bermuda grass, *Cynodon dactylon.*

Sunrise Skipper *Adopaeoides prittwitzi*
   GRASS FAMILY, Poaceae: knot grass, *Paspalum distichum.*

Fiery Skipper *Hylephila phyleus*
   GRASS FAMILY, Poaceae: Bermuda grass, *Cynodon dactylon;* Kentucky bluegrass, *Poa
   pratensis.*

Morrison's Skipper *Stinga morrisoni*
   Host plant not known in Arizona.

Common Branded Skipper *Hesperia comma susanae*
   GRASS FAMILY, Poaceae: red fescue, *Festuca rubra;* blue grama, *Bouteloua gracilis;*
   Muhlenbergia sp.

Juba Skipper *Hesperia juba*
   GRASS FAMILY, Poaceae: Kentucky bluegrass, *Poa pratensis;* slender hairgrass,
   Deschampsia elongata; needlegrass, *Stipa* sp.; red brome, *Bromus rubens.*

Rhesus Skipper *Polites rhesus*
   GRASS FAMILY, Poaceae: blue grama, *Bouteloua gracilis.*

Uncas Skipper *Hesperia uncas*
   GRASS FAMILY, Poaceae: blue grama, *Bouteloua gracilis.*

Nevada Skipper *Hesperia nevada*
   GRASS FAMILY, Poaceae: bottlebrush squirreltail, *Elymus elymoides (=Sitanion hystrix);*
   sheep fescue, *Festuca ovina.*

Carus Skipper *Polites carus*
   Host plant unknown in Arizona—probably grasses.

Green Skipper *Hesperia viridis*
   GRASS FAMILY, Poaceae: blue grama, *Bouteloua gracilis;* sideoats grama, *Bouteloua cor-
   tipendula;* slim tridens, *Tridens muticus;* buffalo grass, *Buchloe dactyloides.*

Pahaska Skipper *Hesperia pahaska*
   GRASS FAMILY, Poaceae: blue grama, *Bouteloua gracilis.*

Apache Skipper *Hesperia woodgatei*
   Host plant not known in Arizona—probably grasses.

Sachem *Atalopedes campestris*
   GRASS FAMILY, Poaceae: Bermuda grass, *Cynodon dactylon;* red fescue, *Festuca rubra;*
   crab grass, *Digitaria sanguinalis.*

Sandhill Skipper *Polites sabuleti*
   GRASS FAMILY, Poaceae: Bermuda grass, *Cynodon dactylon;* Kentucky bluegrass,*Poa
   pratensis.*

Lindsey's Skipper *Hesperia lindseyi*
   Host plant not known in Arizona—probably grasses.

Peck's Skipper *Polites peckius*
   GRASS FAMILY, Poaceae: Kentucky bluegrass,*Poa pratensis;* rice cutgrass, *Leersia oryzoides.*

Taxiles Skipper *Poanes taxiles*
   GRASS FAMILY, Poaceae: Kentucky bluegrass, *Poa pratensis;* Nuttall alkali grass, *Puccinellia
   airoides;* quackgrass, *Elymus smithii;* orchard grass, *Dactylis glomerata;* Canada wild rye,
   Elymus canadensis.

Draco Skipper *Polites draco*
   Host plant not known in Arizona—probably grasses.

Tawny-edged Skipper *Polites themistocles*
GRASS FAMILY, Poaceae: Kentucky bluegrass, *Poa pratensis.*

Sonoran Skipper *Polites sonora sonora*
Host plant not kown in Arizona—probably grasses.

Long Dash *Polites mystic*
GRASS FAMILY, Poaceae: quackgrass, *Elymus repens;* barnyard grass, *Echinochloa crus-galli;* timothy, *Phleum pratense.*

Woodland Skipper *Ochlodes sylvanoides*
GRASS FAMILY, Poaceae: Bermuda grass, *Cynodon dactylon;* wild rye, *Elymus cimereus.*

Delaware Skipper *Anatrytone logan*
GRASS FAMILY, Poaceae: big bluestem, *Andropogon gerardi;* switchgrass, *Panicum virgatum.*

Yuma Skipper *Ochlodes yuma*
GRASS FAMILY, Poaceae: common reed, *Phragmites communis.*

Umber Skipper *Poames melane*
GRASS FAMILY, Poaceae: tufted hair grass, *Deschampsia caespitosa;* Bermuda grass, *Cynopdon dactylon;* California brome, *Bromus carinatus;* goldentop, *Lamarkia aurea.*

Snow's Skipper *Paratrytone snowi*
GRASS FAMILY, Poaceae: pine dropseed, *Blepharoneuron tricholepsis.*

Dun Skipper *Euphyes vestris*
SEDGE FAMILY, Cyperaceae: sedge, *Carex geophila.*

Deva skipper *Atrytonopsis deva*
Host plant not known in Arizona—probably grasses.

Moon-marked Skipper *Atrytonopsis lunus*
GRASS FAMILY, Poaceae: Probably bullgrass, *Muhlenbergia emersleyi.*

White-barred Skipper *Atrytonopsis pittacus*
Host plant not known—probably grasses.

Python Skipper *Atrytonopsis python*
Host plant not known—probably grasses.

Cestus Skipper *Atrytonopsis cestus*
Host plant not known—probably grasses.

Sheep Skipper *Atrytonopsis edwardsii*
GRASS FAMILY, Poaceae: sideoats grama, *Bouteloua curtipendula.*

Bronze Roadside-Skipper *Amblyscirtes aenus*
GRASS FAMILY, Poaceae: sideoats grama, *Bouteloua curtipendula;*

Simius Roadside-Skipper *Amblyscirtes simius*
GRASS FAMILY, Poaceae: blue grama, *Bouteloua gracilis.*

Large Roadside-Skipper *Amblyscirtes exoteria*
GRASS FAMILY, Poaceae: bullgrass, *Muhlenbergia emersleyi.*

Cassus Roadside-Skipper *Amblyscirtes cassus*
GRASS FAMILY, Poaceae: bulb panicum, *Panicum bulbosum.*

Oslar's Roadside-Skipper *Amblyscirtes oslari*
GRASS FAMILY, Poaceae: Host plant unknown in Arizona—sideoats grama, *Bouteloua curtipendula,* used elsewhere.

Texas Roadside-Skipper *Amblyscirtes texanae*
GRASS FAMILY, Poaceae: bulb panicum, *Panicum bulbosum.*

Toltec (Prenda) Roadside-Skipper *Amblyscirtes tolteca*
Host plant not known—probably grasses.

Dotted Roadside-Skipper *Amblyscirtes eos*
GRASS FAMILY, Poaceae: vine mesquite, *Panicum obtusum.*

Elissa Roadside-Skipper *Amblyscirtes elissa*
GRASS FAMILY, Poaceae: sideoats grama, *Bouteloua curtipendula.*

Slaty Roadside-Skipper *Amblyscirtes nereus*
Host plant not known—probably grasses.

Nysa Roadside-Skipper *Amblyscirtes nysa*
 GRASS FAMILY, Poaceae: crabgrass, *Digitaria* spp. including *Digitaria sanguinalis; Paspalum* sp.
Common Roadside-Skipper *Amblyscirtes vialis*
 Host plant not known—probably grasses.
Orange-edged Roadside-Skipper *Amblyscirtes fimbriata*
 GRASS FAMILY, Poaceae: nodding brome, *Bromus anomalus;* Arizona wheatgrass, *Agropyron arizonicum (=Elymus arizonicus).*
Eufala Skipper *Lerodea eufala*
 GRASS FAMILY, Poaceae: Bermuda grass, *Cynodon dactylon;* Johnson grass, *Sorghum halepense.*
Olive-clouded Skipper *Lerodea dysaules*
 GRASS FAMILY, Poaceae: Bermuda grass, *Cynodon dactylon;* green spangletop *Leptochloa dubia.*
Orange-headed Roadside-Skipper *Amblyscirtes phylace*
 GRASS FAMILY, Poaceae: big bluestem, *Andropogon gerardii* and probably other grasses.
Brazilian Skipper *Calpodes ethlius*
 CANNA FAMILY, Cannaceae: common canna, *Canna generalis.*
Orange Giant-Skipper *Agathymus neumoegeni*
 AGAVE FAMILY, Agavaceae: Parry's agave, *Agave parryi.*
Poling's Giant-Skipper *Agathymus polingi*
 AGAVE FAMILY, Agavaceae: shindagger, *Agave schotti;* Toumey's agave, *Agave toumeyana.*
Arizona Giant-Skipper *Agathymus aryxna*
 AGAVE FAMILY, Agavaceae: Palmer's agave, *Agave palmeri;* desert agave, *Agave deserti.*
Huachuca Giant-Skipper *Agathymus evansi*
 AGAVE FAMILY, Agavaceae: Huachuca agave, *Agave parryi* var. *huachucensis.*
Mojave Giant-Skipper *Agathymus alliae*
 AGAVE FAMILY, Agavaceae: Kaibab agave, *Agave utahensis* var. *kaibabensis.*
Yucca Giant-Skipper *Megathymus yuccae*
 AGAVE FAMILY, Agavaceae: Joshua tree, *Yucca brevifolia;* banana yucca, *Yucca baccata;* shindagger, *Yucca schottii;* Mohave yucca, *Yucca shidigera;* Bailey yucca, *Yucca baileyi;* Harriman yucca, *Yucca harrimaniae;* Thornber yucca, *Yucca thornberi.*
Ursine Giant-Skipper *Megathymus ursus*
 AGAVE FAMILY, Agavaceae: shindagger, *Yucca schottii;* banana yucca, *Yucca baccata;* Arizona yucca, *Yucca arizonica;* Thornber yucca, *Yucca thornberi.*
Strecker's Giant-Skipper *Megathymus streckeri*
 AGAVE FAMILY, Agavaceae: Bailey yucca, *Yucca baileyi (=Yucca navajoa);* narrowleaf yucca, *Yucca angustissima.*

Bibliography

Allen, Tom and James P. Brock, *in press*. **Butterfly Caterpillars of Western North America**

Bailowitz, Richard A. and James P. Brock, 1991. **Butterflies of Southeastern Arizona**, Sonoran Arthropod Studies, Inc.

Bailowitz, Richard and Douglas Danforth, 1997. **Common Butterflies of the Southwest**, Southwest Parks and Monuments, Assoc.

Burns, John M. *Pyrgus communis* and *Pyrgus albescens* (Hesperidae: Pyrginae) are Seperate Transcontinental Species with Variable but Diagnostic Values. Journal of the Lepidopterists' Society 54 (2) 2000, 52-71

Cassie, et al, 2001, **North American Butterfly Association (NABA) Checklist and English Names of North American Butterflies**

Desert Butterfly Gardening, 1996. Arizona Native Plant Society and Sonoran Arthropod Studies, Inc.

Epple, Anne O., 1995, **A Field Guide to the Plants of Arizona**, Falcon Publishing, Inc.

Garth, John S. and J. W. Tilden, 1986. **California Butterflies**, University of California Press

Glassberg, Jeffrey, 1999. **Butterflies Through Binoculars: The East**, Oxford University Press

Glassberg, Jeffrey, 2001. **Butterflies Through Binoculars: The West**, Oxford University Press

Gould, Frank 1951. **Grasses of the Southwestern United States**, University of Arizona Press

Kearney, Thomas H. and Robert H. Peebles, 1959. **Arizona Flora**, University of Arizona Press

Opler, Paul A. and Amy Bartlett Wright, 1999. **Western Butterflies**, Houghton Mifflin

Pyle, Robert M., 1981. **The Audubon Society Field Guide to North American Butterflies**, Alfred A. Knopf

Pyle, Robert M. 1984. **Handbook for Butterfly Watchers**, Houghton Mifflin

Scott, James A., 1986. **The Butterflies of North America**, Stanford University Press

Smith, Michael J. and James P. Brock, 1988. A Review of the *Thessalia leanira* Complex in the Southwestern United States (Nyphalidae: Melitaeinae) with a Description of two new sub-species of *Thessalia fulvia*. Bulletin of the Allyn Museum No. 118

Stewart, Bob, 1997. **Common Butterflies of California**, West Coast Lady Press

Waldbauer, Gilbert, 2000. **Millions of Monarchs, Bunches of Beetles**, Harvard University Press

Photographic Credits

Rick and Nora Bowers: 71a, 131a, 273c

Jim Brock: 13a, 13b, 29b, 63c, 65a, 69a, 73c, 87b, 89a, 91b, 91c, 93a, 129b, 135c, 141a, 141b, 143a, 151a, 215a, 223b, 259a, 275b, 277d, 281d, 283a, 289b, 313a, 315a, 321a, 327a,355a, 363b,375b

Priscilla Brodkin: Front Cover, 9, 11a, 11b, 25, 27a, 27b, 37, 39a, 43a, 43b, 45a, 45b, 47a, 51a, 51d, 61a, 83, 85a, 87c, 109c, 113a, 113b, 113c, 115a, 115b, 121a, 127b, 135b, 147a, 149a, 153a, 153c, 157a, 171a, 181a, 181b, 197a, 201b, 211a, 211b, 229a, 229b, 235a, 235b, 237a, 237b, 237d, 239d, 245b, 247b, 249a, 261c, 267b, 271a, 287b, 307a, 307b, 309a, 309b, 311a, 313c, 315d, 317b, 321b, 323a, 323b, 323c, 323d, 325a, 325b, 329a, 335a, 349c, 357c, 359c, 359d, 361a, 361b, 365a, 365b, 365c, 379d, Back Cover - bottom

Cathy Burges: 359a

Robert Campbell: 75b

Doug Danforth: 41a, 65b, 65c, 129a, 161b, 249c, 251a, 259b, 267c, 267d, 275c, 287a, 289c, 311d, 313b, 315c, 359b, 361d, 367c, 373b 373d, 375c, 375d, 379a

Jeff Glassberg: 161a, 161c, 167a, 167b, 251c, 253a, 253b, 255a, 255b,257c, 257d, 269a, 271c, 271d, 297a, 297b, 299a, 299c, 299d, 309c, 309d, 317c, 325c, 327c, 355b, 355c, 377d, 381b, 383b

Jerry McWilliams: 55a, 55b

Paul Opler and Evi Buckner: 133a, 133b, 159c, 169c, 169d, 217c, 299b, 317d, 325d, 327b, 373a, 377b

Mike Quinn: 381a

Larry Sansone: 319a

Bob Stewart: 15a, 15b, 17a, 17b, 19a, 19b, 21, 23a, 23b, 27c, 27d, 29a, 29c, 29d, 31a, 31b, 31c, 33, 35a, 35b, 35c, 39b, 39c, 41b, 41c, 41d, 47b, 49a, 49b, 51b, 51c, 53a, 53b, 53c, 55c, 55d, 57a, 57b, 57c, 59, 61b, 61c, 63a, 63b, 67a, 67b, 67c, 69b, 69c, 71b, 71c, 73a, 73b, 75a, 75c, 75d, 77, 79a, 79b, 79c, 79d, 81a, 81b, 85b, 85c, 87a, 89b, 89c, 89d, 91a, 93b, 93c, 95a, 95b, 95c, 97a, 97b, 97c, 97d, 99, 101a, 101b, 101c, 101d, 103a, 103b, 103c, 103d, 105, 107a, 111a, 111b, 111c, 111d, 117, 119a, 119b, 121b, 123, 125a, 125b,127a, 131b, 135a, 137a, 137b, 139a, 139b, 143b, 145a, 145b, 147b, 149b, 151b, 151c, 153b, 155a, 155b, 157b, 157c, 157d, 159a, 159b, 163a, 163b, 163c, 165a, 165b, 165c, 167c, 169a, 169b, 171b, 171c, 171d, 173a, 173b, 173c, 175a, 175b, 177a, 177b, 179a, 179b, 179c 179d, 183a, 183b, 185a, 185b, 187a, 187b, 189a, 189b, 191a, 191b, 193a, 193b, 195a, 195b, 197b, 199a, 199b, 201a, 203a, 203b, 205a, 205b, 207a, 207b, 209a, 209b, 209c, 213a, 213b, 213c, 215b, 215c, 217a, 217b, 219a, 219b, 221a, 221b, 225a, 225b, 227a, 227b, 231, 233a, 233b, 233c, 233d, 237c, 239a, 239b, 239c, 241, 243a, 243b, 243c, 243d, 245a, 245c, 245d, 247a, 247c, 249b, 251b, 251c, 255c, 255d, 257a, 257b, 259c, 261a, 261b, 261d, 263a, 263b, 263c, 263d, 265a, 265b, 265c, 267a, 269b, 269c, 269d, 271b, 273a, 273b, 275a, 277a, 277b, 277c, 279a, 279b, 279c, 281a, 281b, 281c, 283b, 283c, 285a, 285b, 285c, 285d, 287c, 287d, 289a, 291a, 291b, 291c, 293a, 293b, 293c, 295a, 295b, 295c, 297c, 297d, 301a, 301b, 301c, 301d, 303a, 303b, 303c, 303d, 305a, 305b, 305c, 305d, 307c, 307d, 311b, 311c, 313d, 315b, 317a, 319b, 319c, 329b, 329c, 329d, 331a, 331b, 331c, 331d, 333a, 333b, 333c, 333d, 335b, 335c, 335d, 337a, 337b, 337c, 337d, 339a, 339b, 339c, 339d, 341a, 341b, 341c, 341d, 343a, 343b, 343c, 343d, 345a, 345b, 345c, 345d, 347a, 347b, 347c, 347d, 349a, 349b, 351a, 351b, 351c, 351d, 353a, 353b, 353c, 353d, 357a, 357b, 357c, 357d, 361c, 363a, 363c, 363d, 365d, 367a, 367b, 369a, 369b, 369c, 369d, 371a, 371b, 371c, 371d, 373c, 375a, 377a, 377b, 377c, 379c, 381c, 381d, 383a, 383c, Back Cover top

Index

Number shown in **boldface** type is the page where a species account is found.